658

£7.19

The Self-reliant Manager

SELF-DEVELOPMENT FOR MANAGERS

A major new series of workbooks for managers edited by Jane Cranwell-Ward

This series presents a selection of books in workbook format, on a range of key management issues and skills. The books are designed to provide practising managers with the basis for self-development across a wide range of industries and occupations.

Each book relates to other books in the series to provide a coherent new approach to self-development for managers. Closely based on the latest management training initiatives, the books are designed to complement management development programmes, in-house company training, and management qualification programmes such as CMS, DMS, MBA and professional qualification programmes.

Other books in the series:

Thriving on Stress
Jane Cranwell-Ward

Managing Change
Colin Carnall

Effective Problem Solving
Dave Francis

Accounting for Managers
Roger Oldcorn

Developing Assertiveness
Anni Townend

Forthcoming:

Step by Step Competitive Strategy
Dave Francis

The series editor **Jane Cranwell-Ward** is the Director of Company Programmes at Henley – The Management College. She is the author of *Managing Stress* (Pan, 1986).

The Self-reliant Manager

Chris Bones

London and New York

First published 1994
by Routledge
11 New Fetter Lane, London EC4P 4EE

Simultaneously published in the USA and Canada
by Routledge
29 West 35th Street, New York, NY 10001

Typeset in Times by Solidus (Bristol) Limited
Printed and bound in Great Britain by
Biddles Ltd, Guildford and King's Lynn

British Library Cataloguing in Publication Data

A catalogue reference for this book is available from the British Library.

ISBN 0–415–07928–4

Library of Congress Cataloging in Publication Data

Bones, Chris, 1958–
  The self-reliant manager / Chris Bones.
      p.   cm. – (Self-development for managers)
  ISBN 0–415–07928–4
  1. Executive ability.   2. Self-reliance.   3. Organizational
change.   I. Title.   II. Series.
HD38.2.B66   1994
658.4′09–dc20
                                              93–16828
                                                  CIP

Contents

— *Figures*

Series editor's preface

The Self-development for Managers Series was created to help managers develop the competencies needed to be effective in a rapidly changing environment. As titles are added, they build on the existing series and help managers prepare for future changes.

As organizations move to the twenty-first century, people become their most important resource. In a competitive environment, people can provide an organization with its competitive advantage. Many books have been written on human resource management, however, and I was therefore very keen for a different approach to be taken.

The Self-reliant Manager provides the manager with a wide-ranging view of issues important to the management of human resources. Additional reading is included for those who require more detailed coverage. Later titles in the series are planned to complement *The Self-reliant Manager* with topics such as the impact of information systems and environmental considerations.

Those managers able to implement the lessons developed here will find themselves empowered, able to take responsibility for themselves and their staff. The book will help the reader to develop a personal strategy within the context of their own organization.

I have worked with Chris Bones on many occasions, creating and providing management development programmes for managers. He has always demonstrated creative ability and he is deeply committed to helping organizations tackle human resource issues in order to achieve their business objectives. This makes him the ideal person to write this book. I am also very pleased to have a practitioner as an author in the series.

Jane Cranwell-Ward
Series Editor

Introduction

This book has been partly brought about by frustration: few managers realize the potential they have to contribute significantly to the development of the organization they work for. How many of us have seen our managers wait for others to act when they could have taken the responsibility for action on themselves? Quite often management in the UK has simply failed to see the relevance of big changes in the society in which it operates. Indeed, when we look to a failing industry or operation, more often than not, it is the quality of the management which is as much in question as the structural or labour problems that are being blamed.

From my own experience in working across four major sectors of industry, both in the UK and abroad, it seems to me that managers at all levels are not encouraged to think. We have developed a race of action-oriented men – and I choose the word 'men' deliberately – for whom thinking time is wasted time. So they fail to think about themselves, their operating environment and the wider environment in which their organization exists to see how best they could build and sustain a significant competitive advantage. By not doing so they often fail to see the significance of the opportunities presented by, say, shifts in public sentiment towards property development, or changes in the demographic structure, or the development of new technology. Thinking time prior to decision-making could be the most profitable investment a manager ever makes.

Of the thousands of decisions made every day very few require the board or senior managers to endorse them. They are made by managers. If we could develop greater self-reliance among managers, to have the confidence and the vision to look at themselves, their organizations and the world around them and to change the decisions they make – and the way they make them – we would improve significantly an organization's ability to perform to the highest potential.

As we progress towards the twenty-first century the major issues that face all of us as managers are primarily those with a significant impact on the management of human resources. It is in this area that many managers lack the confidence to take the lead and to change what they do and how they do it. I may be a solitary voice, but it is my contention that unless we develop a leadership role for managers in the issues surrounding the process of managing people in organizations profits will start to falter – or in some cases will never return.

For too long issues concerned with the management of people have been abdicated to so-called professionals, ignored by many organizations until it was too late, fallen victim to costly consultancies with ready-made solutions to non-existent problems or confronted with all the subtlety of a badly aimed brick.

Management is not often associated with leadership unless it is of the idiosyncratic and capricious kind. Management is still seen as essentially a neutral task, often associated with control and more often than not with containment. This is precisely why we have ended up with human resource strategies that constrain and hinder the development of real business growth. A leading industrialist has recently been quoted as pointing out that many of the UK's aspiring personnel professionals fall into two camps: 'a bunch of American Football addicts who take on the unions, or people who devise labyrinthine, non-incentivising remuneration systems.' Both of these habits are all too accurate reflections of the human resource policies of a fair chunk of British industry.

What is badly needed is leadership from managers. The business successes of the late twentieth and early twenty-first centuries will be those firmly founded on a clear appreciation of the impact of major business issues on the people and the development of strategies to deal with them. This will require us to develop self-reliant managers with the courage to demonstrate leadership in key areas where others may falter, fail to take a risk or refuse to seize the initiative. We fail to appreciate this at our peril.

This book, then, offers itself as a 'primer' for managers, to start the process of considering the major issues facing most organizations as they progress towards the year 2000; to begin to develop greater self-reliance in the area of human resource management. The selection of issues is deliberately biased towards those with a significant impact on the management of people within organizations. If they are not taken seriously and responded to in the next few years they will, I believe, lead to a decline in competitiveness and consequently in profitability.

Profit may seem to some an odd word to emphasize in a book which looks at key people issues. Surely we are about to be bombarded by empty phrases about relationships, motivation, training, maximizing potential, etc.? Well, no doubt there will be some of that – it is, after all, an inescapable trait of my profession. However, the essential point is this: get it right and you can build and sustain real competitive advantage through the effective management of the key resource. As markets get tougher and increasingly global, and as demands for public-sector efficiency increase year on year, the only asset that can give an organization a genuine competitive edge is its people.

We can all make a difference in this area: all of us deal with people, either working with them, for them, or they for us. Much of the impact we have comes from the day-to-day decisions – and implementation of decisions – that we make. Not our superiors, nor the board. So, although the book deals with each issue at a broad level, covering key points, it then goes on to offer practical steps and suggestions. In order to help you generate your own appreciation of what it may mean for your own area each issue has its own stocktake. These aim to help you develop a personal action plan for your area of responsibility as well as considering some broader actions to take forward in your organization – encouraging you to become a self-reliant manager and to take a leadership role within your own organization.

USING THIS BOOK

The book has been designed to be followed through as a whole. Should one issue be of particular interest, however, then the sections are sufficiently self-contained to be used as separate modules. As a self-development workbook it is structured so that it raises a series of related issues and then via simple 'stocktakes' allows you to explore these issues as they relate to you or your business and then to develop action plans. It is also deliberately broad rather than deep, so that whilst issues are raised and discussed, further reading and exploration are indicated in the notes for each chapter should a particular issue be a challenge to your operation.

— *Acknowledgements*

At a time when I changed companies, changed jobs, moved house and moved my family in and out of North America for a brief sojourn, I also agreed to write a book. It can only be thanks to the support and understanding of my wife that I am still alive and married at the end of it. I am also very appreciative of the support, advice and encouragement of Jane Cranwell-Ward. In addition, I would like to thank my colleagues who willingly read and commented on the ideas and their presentation. More formal thanks go to United Distillers for allowing me to reproduce their illustration of organizational culture and for being supportive of this project. I am also very grateful to David Maitland of People in Business for allowing me to reproduce his work on performance reviews.

1 *The self-reliant manager*

To be able to demonstrate leadership, a manager must become self-reliant. By this I mean they must have thought through for themselves the major issues facing their business and their own area of responsibility; and have developed a clear understanding of the impact those issues will have. This self-reliance is the essential prerequisite of leadership.

As we approach the twenty-first century the major issues for management, certainly in Europe and North America, will focus sharply on the management of people as a vital asset. We will hear less and less about the cost associated with employment and more and more about the need to develop skilled and committed employees who can provide the business with a competitive edge. In order to do this effectively managers need to understand themselves, the internal environment of their organization and the external environment in which that organization exists.

UNDERSTANDING YOURSELF

As managers we need a balanced view of ourselves in respect of our performance, our experience, our personal strengths and our development needs. That view needs to come from more sources than the usual one – performance review – and should be placed in the context of what we are trying to achieve in our current role as well as what we would like to see as the future.

It is also true that as managers we are going to have to take the responsibility for managing our own futures. Understanding our future in the light of all the issues raised in the book will place us in

1

the position of thinking ahead of developments rather than reacting to them.

As organizations change, as numbers of people diminish and breadth of responsibilities widen so we are going to need to develop different skills in order to manage successfully. These will have less to do with direct line management of people and more to do with managing issues through others with whom we work or who report to other people.

UNDERSTANDING THE INTERNAL ENVIRONMENT

As the traditional recruiting pools reduce right across Europe and North America so the challenge for us is to bring new groups into the mainstream workforce. Doing this will force us to reconsider the traditional patterns of work which have dominated the public and private sectors for the last sixty years or so.

As organizations flatten out and slim down, more and more of us will be working in roles that involve working across teams or departments rather than running them. We will need to work in temporary teams and informal groups and to find ways of gaining acceptance of decisions that do not necessarily follow the traditional line structure. We will have to learn to manage less through control and more through generating and maintaining individual commitment.

As organizations progress they will also have to learn continuously. To learn from change – which will be the only likely constant – from the past, from others. This will require considerable shifts in systems and processes, in management attitudes to risk and to training and development, which will have to become less concerned with formal off-the-job programmes and more with on-the-job coaching and learning.

The pace of change and the requirements to learn will finally give the full potential of information systems a chance to build real competitive advantage. The impact on a business of 're-engineering' its processes, allowing individuals to develop greater responsibilities and generate commitment throughout an organization, could be dramatic. We will need, however, to learn to break the rules we have already and not automate what exists: we will need to develop new approaches to the management and use of information.

Real competitive edge will come from people fulfilling their highest potential in those areas where the business needs to have the highest quality. The identification of the core skills necessary to succeed will be an essential prerequisite of growth in the twenty-first century. Given this, it is important that standards are set, measured and rewarded in a positive manner.

UNDERSTANDING THE EXTERNAL ENVIRONMENT

Many of these internal organizational developments are in themselves the result of changes in the external environments in which we all operate. The impact that shifts in the demographics of Europe and North America will have on us will mean that we will have to diversify our workforce and think more clearly about our recruitment and development policies. Public awareness and concern over the environment have a whole range of implications. These will not only affect potential recruits but have real implications for sales and competitive positioning.

The question of ethics and the conduct of business has been forced very publicly on to our agendas. We will need to ensure that how we conduct ourselves will stand up to external as well as internal scrutiny.

CREATING A CLIMATE OF SUCCESS

Developing responses to these issues and moving towards an environment where management relies far more on commitment from individuals than on control processes will mean an eventual shift in the values of an organization. It will have a significant impact on the culture of the business.

In order to manage successfully we must demonstrate a coherent vision and strong values. We have to give strong leadership to give our businesses a competitive edge. This competitive edge will be based on values that establish people firmly at the centre of the businesses' strategy.

By a value I mean a belief that is being put into action. A value is not a mission statement nor a plaque on the wall. Unless we are seen by those who work for us and those who purchase our goods and services to be living our corporate values we will fail. As managers we also have to realize that personal standards play a large role in this. They can underpin or undermine corporate values. You can have the largest quality department in the world but unless everyone is a quality manager no quality programme can be sustained in the longer term.

Figure 1.1 outlines the structure of the book and how it reflects these broad themes. Each of the chapters starts with a reference to this structure, showing where it fits in the overall picture. The chapters map out the key themes that are facing all of us in this area and provide simple models and prompts that allow exploration of those themes as they apply to the process of management.

Our challenge as managers is to develop a strategy tailored to our own business needs and then to turn our attention to appropriate solutions. We have to understand what is happening in our organizations and establish the gaps that need bridging to generate maximum performance. Regardless of the nature of our business or service, should we as managers fail to provide this leadership, then we will have missed a clear opportunity to establish a competitive advantage in an increasingly tight marketplace.

BEFORE YOU BEGIN

Before you begin it is worth taking stock of where you are now and trying to establish some key objectives and success measurements that you can keep referring to throughout the book.

STOCKTAKE 1: WHERE AM I NOW?

Think about your business and your own department/sector.

■ What are the five major people-based issues facing them at the moment?

Business	*Department/Sector*
1	1
2	2
3	3
4	4
5	5

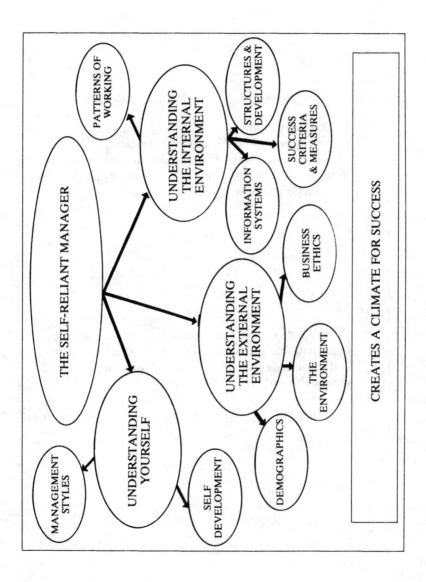

Figure 1.1 The structure and themes of the book

■ Which issues are common to both?

1

2

3

4

5

■ Look at your common issue(s). Try to identify key
themes against those discussed under each of the
sections above. Establish the most important themes by
looking for those which are most commonly involved in
the issue(s) you have identified.

1

2

3

4

5

■ From the themes you have identified, set yourself five
objectives that you would like to have achieved by the
end of working through this book. Establish a
measurable output and a time scale.

Objective	*Output*	*Timing*
1		
2		
3		
4		
5		

You have completed a stocktake of where you are now. From here you can attack this book in one of two ways: either start with the chapters where you feel you will get the most relevant material with which to address your objectives; or be structured, methodical – nay, managerial – and start with the next chapter. Either way, do cover those areas which at first sight do not seem as relevant – you may be surprised!

2 Demographics, diversity and the structure of work

The demographic changes that are unfolding in Europe and North America will have an irreversible impact on the way in which businesses staff their operations and the patterns of work which they employ to gain maximum efficiency. Although economic circumstances may mask the full impact in the shorter term, businesses risk serious disruption if they do not respond by setting themselves up to manage in the longer term.

THE CHALLENGE OF DEMOGRAPHICS

Few popular commentators have really understood the challenge of the demographic shifts that face many Western economies. The absolute shift in numbers is for most economies irrelevant. The key point is this: the 18–24 age bracket is the premier recruitment pool for most businesses and public-sector organizations. Even at current levels of unemployment in the UK all recruiting organizations have been finding it increasingly difficult to obtain the right resource with the right level of qualification. Given that there will be substantially fewer people in the 18–24 pool that has traditionally supplied the bulk of the needs, the number of those with the necessary skills to take business forward will be even smaller. It is this worsening of the skill shortage that is the demographic challenge. A skill shortage that if not addressed imaginatively is likely to affect seriously the ability of some businesses to grow profitably in the longer term.

Admittedly, economic circumstances have forced many companies to reduce their intake from the traditional pool, and unemployment in much of Europe and North America is higher

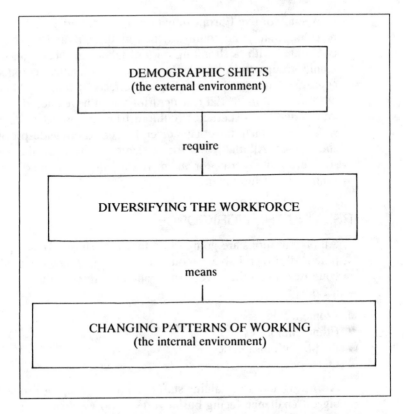

Figure 2.1 The effects of demographic shifts on the structure of work

than in the 1980s. However, even in these times we can see signs that things are changing. In the UK despite increasing numbers of graduates the major graduate recruiters still compete for the same very small pool of well qualified and appropriately skilled 18–24 year olds. All that is happening now, given lower levels of economic activity, is that if a company fails to find the right graduate it will not recruit. It still has to find the right people. As the traditional pool gets smaller it will have to look further afield. When the upturn comes companies will need more of the right people: it is a sad comment on the state of the British education system that most of us are not confident that we will find them from the products of the new university system.

A study of five European nations in 1990 underlined this point, revealing that some countries such as the UK and Germany are confronted with 'a shrinking pool of labour in those age, sex and ethnic groups from which they have traditionally recruited. All countries [surveyed] are feeling the effects of rapid technological advances and industrial restructuring which have altered the skills, knowledge and experience required from almost all categories of staff, and which have concurrently generated widespread skill shortages.'[1] All this calls for a significant shift in the way we structure jobs, recruit for them, reward those recruited and then train and develop them.

DIVERSIFYING THE WORKFORCE

All organizations are going to be forced to shift into new pools of potentially recruitable labour. For the European Community countries and other Western economies these alternative pools include:

- Women
- Ethnic minorities
- People with disabilities
- Older people

Attracting and/or retaining staff from these groups is probably the biggest challenge facing business. How do we diversify the work-force without risking being accused of 'lowering standards' at one extreme or 'tokenism' at the other? It is worth asking why key groups of potentially qualified labour are traditionally excluded either from the managerial/professional/skilled workforce or from the workforce altogether. As a society we have, at times consciously, put up firm barriers for certain of our citizens.

Women

Although a significant part of the business workforce during the first world war, women (with a very few exceptions sprung from the wealthy elite) did not begin to break through the barriers of a male-dominated managerial establishment until fairly recently. Only as the UK came to terms with recovery from the second world war in the late 1950s did women start to progress through the higher education establishments in sufficient numbers to have an impact. Progress has been painfully slow in management – women having found the professions easier to enter – given the 'arts-based' courses many had been led into by the education system.

Even today there are still very obvious barriers to the progress of women to the very top jobs in all organizations. Now in 1993 women head several notable public institutions: the Crown Prosecution Service, the Prime Minister's Policy Unit, Customs and Excise and the Security Service are examples. In the private sector, however, there are very few examples and those that spring to mind, Anita Roddick for example, have done so outside the established corporations. Whether we like it or not, we in the UK operate a very effective 'glass ceiling' through which women rarely pass.

Despite the fine words – remember Opportunity 2000? – very little is actively being done to change the supports that prop up our glass ceilings. The 1991 report from the Europe-wide survey referred to earlier discerned little progress: only a third of employers in the UK monitor the progress of women who are promoted into management jobs. Paternity leave is offered by fewer than one in five organizations. Other benefits such as childcare, childcare allowances and career breaks are even less widespread.[2] These physical arrangements all contribute to reducing barriers: however, they do not address the fundamentals. Why in so many organizations is it unacceptable to work from home when a child is sick?

Ethnic minorities

As each group of immigrants have come to the UK over the centuries so they have been excluded from the mainstream and denied access to advancement and the controlling power groupings in society. Huguenots in the seventeenth century; Eastern European Jews in the eighteenth and nineteenth centuries; the Irish in the nineteenth century – all met with rejection and years of exclusion from all but the lowliest of professions.

The ethnic minority immigrants of the 1950s, 1960s and early 1970s faced the same issues. The key difference for them was, and still is to a great extent, the colour of their skin. It is true of any newcomers to an established grouping that they try to adapt and 'fit in' quickly and, for many, unobtrusively. Previous groups, without denying or rejecting anything of their cultural/ethnic and religious heritage, all managed to achieve this, partly through their lack of obvious external difference. Very few white people in the UK today are actively discriminated against owing to their religion or their ethnic background. Obvious difference breeds immediate difficulties in the eyes of any established organization – it raises fears of behaviour that does not fit the 'norm' and of values that are not common to the 'majority'.

With ethnic minority groups in the UK, particularly those with African or Caribbean antecedents, we are in danger of creating a second-class society with no access to positions of power or influence, either political or economic. Los Angeles in 1992 may have been an American nightmare: we would be foolish not to start to put our own house in order before our society too is faced with the same violent outpourings of hate.

As managers we are all in a position to influence, in many cases directly, the future direction of these groupings in our society. Unless the barriers come down we will never be able to work with the majority of our fellow citizens from minority groups whose greatest desire is for the opportunity to share in the benefits of the generation of wealth.

Whilst this may sound like an uncomfortably political tract in a practical book, remember the challenge facing all of us as managers: from where do we find the skilled workforce we need if we are to continue to succeed against our competitors? Certainly not from a disenchanted, ill educated and disenfranchised under-class.

People with disabilities

It says nothing for industry in the UK that very few organizations reach even the modest 3 per cent target for employees registered as disabled. Access, technology, ignorance and misplaced sympathy are all major issues for many people with disabilities who wish to be given an opportunity to apply their skills. Most of us able-bodied managers when faced with the question 'Could someone with a disability do this job?' immediately look for the difficulties. We fail to remember that, for example, over 80 per cent of people with a disability are not in wheelchairs. Epilepsy and deafness are two of the less obvious examples.

The private sector has such a bad track record with its attitude to employing people with disabilities that most such people do not even bother to scan the standard adverts in, say, the *Sunday Times*. The little government symbol so hastily adopted by some major companies has by that very speed of adoption fallen into disrepute: for little has changed. Why?

Let me give you a personal example. Fired up by participation in Stephen Duckworth's excellent 'Disability Matters' programme,[3] I was presented with the opportunity of a nationwide recruitment exercise for support staff in eight new offices we were opening across England. In order to show our (very genuine) willingness to appoint people with disabilities who met the skill specifications we advertised especially in a paper focused entirely at our target group. Our advert stressed our desire to encourage those with disabilities to apply. We received one application.

On investigation we were left in no doubt why. We were the only private sector organization to advertise there, we had no track record of recruiting and developing people with disabilities, and the reaction from the organizations we approached for help was that most of the people we wanted to attract had so little faith in our sincerity that they would have seen it merely as a paper exercise. 'If you had made 450 applications and never had an interview you would understand it when we say you'll have to reach out much further than that if you are going to persuade us you mean it,' we were told.

The forgotten generations

The boards of directors of the last three companies I have worked for have had average ages of 40–45. In the rest of Europe, North America and Asia Pacific you could add ten years to that average and the boards would still be young. For some reason the UK went on a youth trip during the 1980s and created a pool of under-utilized or unutilized skilled people who form the nucleus of the long-term unemployed. This was exacerbated by the massive shake-outs of the early 1980s when voluntary leaving packages encouraged those over 55 to leave with big pay-outs and early pensions.

It would be difficult for me in particular to criticize the rapid rise of the younger generations throughout much of British industry, particularly the financial, retailing and service sectors. It is, however, difficult to justify a process which merely replaced the dominance of an older generation with what at times can seem to be the tyranny of a younger one. A mix of experience, attitudes and approaches makes for a much healthier business.

Much more important, however, is the reservoir of skill and expertise which we are forgetting about in our haste to pull in bright young graduates from academic institutions. A compulsory retirement age – should any of us get there! – of quite probably 63 in a few years' time also removes vital skills from the workforce much earlier than we need to. As we get more and more stretched to resource skilled workforces so it will become more than evident that to keep the economy going the government will have to introduce a much more flexible retirement system which allows full retirement from say 55 to 75. A consequential introduction by companies of reduced hours/flexible work packages (and this will mean changes to corporate pension schemes in particular) could open up considerable opportunities.

If this sounds a little like a manifesto – long on analysis and short on specifics – at the risk of repeating myself let me stress the key point: unless we remove the barriers, institutional or subconscious, to participation in management as well as general employment we will not succeed in overcoming the skill shortages that we all face over the next ten to fifteen years. If we can't overcome them, then our competition – overseas as well as domestic – will gain the upper hand. So at a practical level what can we do?

ACTION STEPS

Examine selection processes

Most of us use the least effective methods of assessing needs and the suitability of individuals to match those needs: person specifications and general interviews. How many person 'specs' have you seen that seem to hold a mirror to the current incumbent (if successful) or to the manager recruiting the role? Age ranges, experience tracks, educational qualifications, professional memberships all close down options for consideration that could well offer much better matched skills.

When we interview what strikes us first? Certainly not the skills match, rather the presentation, cultural 'fit' and similarities to current role-models. What chance has a non-white male, or an older woman, in these circumstances? If interviews are to be successful then we need to understand the skills we need to perform effectively in a particular role. The most complete approach to this is considered later when we look at the role of competences in management. However, the minimum is that each time a job comes up we should break down the activities into skill sets.

We should then look for a structure in an interview that focuses entirely on the evidence for these skills being present. We can only do this, in an interview, from reviewing past performance. From this we may have some chance of predicting the future; but only some. Stocktake 2 asks you to consider your own role in this respect.

In addition to more structured interviews, tests, assessment exercises that simulate tasks/problems encountered and behaviour predictors are all useful additional information and have the advantage of being more objective than a single interview aimed at looking for the right 'person' rather than the right skills. This is not to say that personality fit and style and team balance are not important: an approach that starts from the positive of 'We have the skills, now let's see if it will work' should, however, open up the pool from which we can choose. Stocktake 3 asks you do this for your own role.

Review performance appraisal/development systems

The way we appraise and the areas that we decide to appraise and give importance to can be significant barriers to the development of women and minority groups in the workforce. What areas does your appraisal system review at present? What emphasis is given to areas that are quite clearly the predominant characteristic of a particular group? Are these balanced by equal emphasis elsewhere? These questions are important when it comes to assessment of the development potential of individuals who do not come from the majority group. How often have we seen behaviour in men complimented as assertive whilst the same behaviour in women is disparaged as aggressive?

The way in which we define key qualities is fundamental to this area. Competences do provide one way forward with neutral definitions that encourage particular behaviours. A key competence should be the ability to manage and work with diversity – this in itself makes a statement which reinforces commitment to removing barriers. The theme is developed later in this book.

Improve managerial awareness

I could have entitled this section 'Attack prejudice', for that is really what it requires; but prejudice more often than not comes from ignorance. Providing knowledge can lift barriers without anyone appearing to be the caped crusader and resident puritan. Getting your peers to understand the reasons for not accepting 'girlie' calendars, for not suffering sexist or racist jokes/comments in the workplace is a whole lot easier if they are confronted in a positive way through awareness training rather than by you acting the moral guardian.

Providing positive reinforcement through career development, training and remuneration for positive behaviour in this, as in any other, respect will also aid the change process. We will never attract and retain high-quality women, ethnic minorities or people with disabilities unless we demonstrate that we are genuinely equal opportunity employers – if we fail to do this we limit our skills base unnecessarily.

Support the change agents

Until organizations develop successful diversity management processes it is likely that we will need to consider special training/ development support for those we initially appoint to key roles, from whichever of the groups above they come from. Certainly the idea of women's networks in organizations and women-only training is gaining ground in some areas and this may be one effective response.

It is certainly true that focusing on key groups in formal development reviews/succession planning activity, etc., can aid the eradication of barriers. Support training/mentoring on how to operate in the new environment and how to balance all the new demands with home, physical or other pressures would also aid success and help to develop positive role models to build upon.

STOCKTAKE 2: SKILLS AND UNBIASED ASSESSMENT

Devising a skills specification

■ First make a note of the major tasks you are required to carry out:

1

2

3

4

5

6

7

8

■ What skills do they require of you?

1 Technical/professional (e.g. financial, legal, computing, etc.)

2 Critical/analytical (e.g. data numerate, quantitative techniques, interpretation of data, etc.)

3 Reporting (e.g. presentations, written reports)

4 Managerial/supervisory (e.g. setting goals, appraising, budget management, etc.)

5   Interpersonal (e.g. communications, relationships, etc.)

6   Other

Structuring the interview

You now have a basic skill specification. The headings are mine and should be changed if you feel you have a better split or already use skill sets/competences with which you are comfortable. Now take each skill set and, looking for the most important area in each set, develop a structured interview process using the following framework. I will take the example of communication skills:

Q   Can you give me an example from your own experience where you have been required to apply your communication skills in order to achieve a specific goal or target?
    Note the answer – you will use it later.
Q   How did you go about this ... (whatever)?
    As above.
Q   What was the impact of your own contribution?
    As above.
Q   Were communications skills appraised in the organization you were/are working for?
    As above.
Q   If so, what was your last assessment?
    As above.
Q   How would your colleagues/subordinates rate your ability in this area?
    As above.

Ideally you should have no more than six key skills you wish to explore. Now find a colleague or friend and conduct your interview. Even better, get them to interview you in their normal way as a comparison.

Assessing the evidence

What have you got? Try mapping out the evidence you have
accumulated under each of your skill sets.

Skill	Positive evidence	Match to original specification
1		
2		
3		
4		
5		
6		

Having mapped out the evidence, now compare it with the
original spec. You have probably accumulated a great deal
of very relevant data which will clearly point towards a
degree of suitability.

Compare the data accumulated by your colleague/friend.
The chances are – unless they are very skilled – that they too
have a great deal but they may have missed some key areas.
Which set of data would give you the best-quality decision?
How are you now going to use this in your organization?

STOCKTAKE 3: REMOVING BARRIERS

Look at your skills specification again. Ask yourself the following:

■   What equipment do I use?

1
2
3
4
5
etc.

■   What special training have I had?

1
2
3
4
5
etc.

■   Where do I carry out my job?

1
2
3
4
5
etc.

■   What special characteristics are required to be successful in my job?

1
2
3
4
5
etc.

■ How would I define the culture in which I work, e.g. the company values and management style?

1
2
3
4
5
etc.

■ Taking each of the areas above, consider blockages for the following groups:

Blockage	Women	Ethnic minority men/ women	People with disabilities	Over-50s
Equipment				
Training				
Physical environment				
Character				
Culture				

■ Take each blockage you have identified and develop an action plan or set of ideas to remove it:

	Blockage	*Action*
1		
2		
3		
4		
5		

etc.

■ Now set yourself a goal to implement those actions which you believe are either yours to decide or those upon which you could influence others to decide.

	Action plan	*Timing*
1		
2		
3		
4		
5		

etc.

■ How will you address the rest?

1
2
3
4
5
etc.

CHANGING THE STRUCTURE OF WORK

The traditional structure and patterns of work are going to be eroded as we progress through the 1990s. Attracting recruits from more diverse backgrounds than the traditional WASP male starts to have an impact on the role that we ask them to perform and on the way in which they make their contribution to the business. On top of this all groups in society – certainly in Western European economies – are starting to attach greater importance to other activities than 'work'. This demand for greater leisure time is partly fuelled by a general reduction in working hours and by greater prosperity, which starts to move people from being concerned with the basics of day-to-day survival towards a concern with the quality of life.

It is going to be increasingly difficult to find totally mobile managers, for example. In the age of dual careers, and of a greater value placed on children's education, neither female nor male managers will be so willing to move at the drop of a hat. Average working hours will also be affected – particularly in the management cadre. Those with family responsibilities as well as those who have commitments equal to those at work will not be as willing to work regular twelve-to-fourteen-hour days as their predecessors in the times of a plentiful supply of qualified labour.

Bringing into the workplace people with disabilities, women with families and people from ethnic minority groups will all require a new approach to working hours, times and environments. The Europe-wide trends study for 1991[4] found that in every country there was a definable increase in flexible working patterns in response to changing demographic pressures, increased competition and reduced public spending. The most common of these flexible patterns was part-time working.

This need not just be reduced hours or fewer than five days per week. In the UK in 1990/91 McDonalds ran a highly publicized campaign to recruit mothers with school-age children by offering school-term contracts working from 10.00 a.m. to 3.00 p.m., five days per week – a time when their other part-timers, school-children over 16, students, vacation workers, etc., were not available for work.

As a variant of part-time working, job-sharing has continued to increase, but from a very low base. It is still not very common outside the public sector but has immense potential. I have used it successfully as a way of bringing maternity returners back into the workforce in secretarial positions. They worked a two-day/three-day split alternating every week with no disruption to the depart-ment and probably more productively than a single individual.

Working practices still in their infancy but used in some organizations are annual hours contracts – which have consider-able potential in shiftwork or areas with highly seasonal workloads – and homebasing. British Telecom's experiment with Directory Enquiry staff, basing them at home with computer terminal and telephone links, will be closely studied as a possible model.

A final area that applies to the management level in organiz-ations is that of executive leasing or the utilizing of temporary executives for particular projects or to cover roles whilst recruit-ment takes place. Not only are there cost savings to companies which go down this route, but there are advantages to individuals, who can choose their length of employment and the organizations for which they work with far greater ease than those of us committed full-time to one company.

So, if we have to change our tried and tested methods, we are going to have to change our traditional view of how we structure roles in our organizations. Of course we all think we are not only indispensable but also that ours is the only way in which our responsibilities can be successfully carried out. However untenable a job-share or part-time contract is at present, the option of restructuring a role and performing as efficiently, if not more so, may well provide us with a way of meeting the challenge to expand our qualified workforce.

STOCKTAKE 4: CHANGING THE STRUCTURE OF JOBS

Take the key functions which you outlined in Stocktake 2.

■ Taking each function, allocate a proportion of time that you spend attending to that function, taking your overall job-activity time as 100 per cent.

	Function	*Percentage time*
1		
2		
3		
4		
5		
6		

■ Taking each proportion in size order, split these percentages down by the type of activity below.

Activity	1	2	3	4	5	6	*Total*
Thinking/planning							
Talking on phone							
Writing/reading							
Trips to customers, suppliers, etc.							

Meetings

Total

■ Now draw a pie chart to show how much time you
spend on each activity (Figure 2.2). Answer the
following:

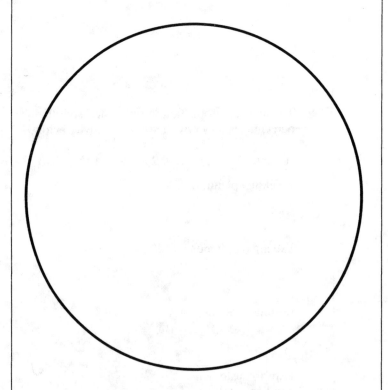

Figure 2.2 Pie chart showing activity split

- How often do I *need* to be in my office/plant, etc.?

  Under 20 per cent
  20–40 per cent
  41–60 per cent
  61–80 per cent
  Over 80 per cent

- How many of these activities need a single person to carry them out to ensure success?

  Under 20 per cent
  20–40 per cent
  41–60 per cent
  61–80 per cent
  Over 80 per cent

- How many of these activities need executing within my current standard hours of work?

  Under 20 per cent
  20–40 per cent
  41–60 per cent
  61–80 per cent
  Over 80 per cent

- What happens when I go on vacation or am absent or on sick leave?

- Now consider your responses. Could your role successfully be executed in another way?

  Part-time
  Job-share
  Flexitime
  Annual hours contract
  Homebased

■ Now consider other roles in the department, particularly those over which you can have some influence when they come up for resourcing. Which roles could be structured differently, what actions e.g. installing technology at home, are required and is there more than one option?

Role	Option 1	Action	Option 2	Action
1				
2				
3				
4				
5				

etc.

■ Now, for the real challenge ... go sell these to your HR department!

3 Continuous development and the need to learn

As the desire for greater quality of life continues to increase and people strive for personal satisfaction, so there will be an ever increasing demand from individuals that organizations provide them with opportunities for personal growth. The impact of the demographic squeeze will put increasing pressure on companies to provide them. Not only this but as competition stiffens the companies that survive will be those which can develop organizations where learning is a continuous process throughout an individual's employment. As a recent report put it: 'Our hopes of health, wealth and happiness depend on learning – our own and that of others.'[1] By personal growth I mean development that is not necessarily work-related but is adding to the sum of the individual and therefore allows them to operate on a wider sphere; for example, the acquisition of language skills.

The UK has a thriving sub-culture of adult learning outside the workplace: evening classes, educational holidays, sports coaching and most obvious of all the Open College and Open University are all testament to this. Paradoxically, formal learning for the vast majority of school/college age children stops at one of the lowest average ages of all EC countries. What stops here, and is rarely taken up voluntarily again, is the learning of basic skills that provide the foundation for the advanced skills so desperately required by all sectors to sustain and grow their businesses. As long as we continue to fail to attack this basic problem we will continue to enhance the impact of the shortage of people from whom we can select the right skills for the 1990s.

The other incongruity is that we have failed to recognize that if we harnessed this willingness to learn and transferred it to the

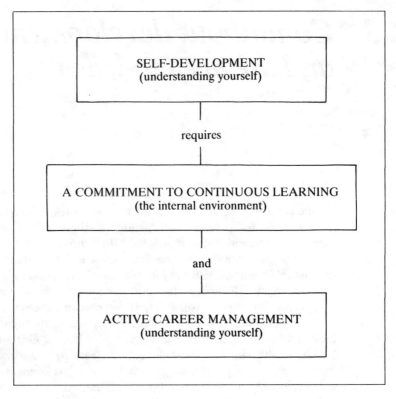

Figure 3.1 Self-development and the need to learn

workplace we could begin the process of empowering those who work in our organizations to take charge of their own development. It is my contention that by doing this we could start to meet what one company chairman called 'The challenge of getting extraordinary performance from ordinary people'. A challenge that has to be met if our businesses are to grow in the 1990s.

For learning is light years away from training. It covers job-related, business related and personal growth. It considers an individual as a complete person, rather than as an accountant, or plant manager – which can only be a part of the whole. Fundamentally it is based on an enhanced ability to learn through experience – both one's own and that of others. Learning, and development through the application of learning, is the theme of this section. Before we look at other people and organizations, however, let's start by looking at self-development and the need to understand oneself.

SELF-DEVELOPMENT – TAKING CHARGE OF YOUR OWN DEVELOPMENT

How well do you know yourself? Having written this down, it looks a little like the start to a *Cosmopolitan* questionnaire headlined 'How hot are you this summer?' For all that, it is still valid. It is only if you can appreciate your own skills base and the gaps there may be in it against your current role requirements that you can even begin to consider taking charge of your own development.

This is also true of those who work for you. If you can get them to *own* their personal development needs, the action you can develop jointly will be twice as powerful in addressing those needs and, eventually, improving performance. This presumption is based on the simple observation that an individual who comes up with their own idea for improvement is far more likely to see it through to the end, and to employ the new skills they have acquired on a regular basis. How many people do you know who have taken up golf later in life and are out in all weathers as they try to improve their handicap? If we can transfer the same enthusiasm to the workplace we can generate immense leaps in individual performance.

The first stage in effecting such a transfer is to review strengths and areas where development may be required. To do this properly requires a skills audit.

STOCKTAKE 5: WHAT WAS IT I WAS GOOD AT ANYWAY?

■ Think back over your last ten years or so. Select up to four key achievements of which you are particularly proud and four incidents where you failed to achieve a goal. You should consider both work and leisure activities. Now complete the following:

Achievement 1

What was your
achievement?

How did you achieve it?

What skills did you use?

Achievement 2

What was your
achievement?

How did you achieve it?

What skills did you use?

Achievement 3

What was your
achievement?

How did you achieve it?

What skills did you use?

Achievement 4

What was your
achievement?

How did you achieve it?

What skills did you use?

Incident 1

What did you try to
achieve?

Incident 2

What did you try to
achieve?

Why did you fail?   Why did you fail?

What skills did you lack?   What skills did you lack?

Incident 3   *Incident 4*

What did you try to   What did you try to
achieve?   achieve?

Why did you fail?   Why did you fail?

What skills did you lack?   What skills did you lack?

■ Review your achievements. Which skills appear more
than once?

1
2
3
4
5
etc.

■ Review your failures. What skills could you have applied to succeed?

1
2
3
4
5
etc.

■ In the two lists are there any surprises? If so, why?

1
2
3
4
5
etc.

■ Do any appear in both lists? Why?

1
2
3
4
5
etc.

■ Now take your lists and do a reality check. Share them with a friend outside work, with a colleague and with any formal feedback you have had at work, e.g. an appraisal. Start with your skill list

Your skill list	*Friend skill list*	*Colleague skill list*	*Appraisal skill list*
1			
2			
3			
4			
5			
etc.			

■ If other skills not on your list are brought to your
   attention, ask for evidence and record it here

1
2
3
4
5
etc.

■ Now move to areas you have identified for development
   through your issues list

Your dev'ment list	Friend dev'ment list	Colleague dev'ment list	Appraisal dev'ment list

1
2
3
4
5
etc.

Note here any issues not on your list and record
evidence given to support them

1
2
3
4
5
etc.

Having considered yourself, and having sought feedback
and checked out your own view, you should have a
pretty fair idea of your strengths and those areas where
you should concentrate for your development. All these
have been backed up with evidence and therefore have a
context which will be very helpful when considering
exactly how you could go about addressing the
development needs and building on the strengths. So as
a recap:

	Strengths	Development needs
1		
2		
3		
4		
5		
6		
7		
8		

NB. You do not have to find eight of either!
What you have just completed could be regarded as
an extended self-appraisal – it is just that, instead of one
year with all its extenuating circumstances and particular
emphases, you have looked at a time period large
enough to iron out the glitches and to see the key trends
and the underlying themes. These are what make or
break effective development. Hence the question 'How
well do you know yourself?'

MAKING THE MOVE FROM TRAINING TO LEARNING

A recent article pointed out that 'any company that aspires to
succeed in the tougher business environment of the 1990s must
first resolve a basic dilemma: success in the marketplace increasingly depends on learning, yet most people don't know how to
learn'.[2] As pointed out earlier, we can all show very positive
learning skills outside work. The barrier for most people is not in
developing learning skills, it is reducing the perceived risks of
admitting a lack of knowledge or expertise. Just think for a
moment about your own skills analysis.

There were no doubt areas of development that you were quite
comfortable in admitting to. In my experience of listening to
management assessments the most common of these are: needing
to pay more attention to detail, not tolerating fools easily, taking
risks without enough to back the judgement, speaking your mind,
etc. These are some of the 'acceptable' management weaknesses.
The ones we forgive, that are allowable in some way or other.

Then, of course, there were those (if you and your informants were open and honest) that were rather more difficult. No one likes to think that they are regarded as not particularly creative, as a poor communicator, a weak team player, a bad listener or some other such thing. These failings are more difficult to admit and, therefore, more difficult to address.

In the work context, particularly as you rise through the management structures, placing yourself in a position where you may expose a weakness is still seen as an unacceptable risk by most managers. Yet much of what we need to learn from experience – either our own or that of others – is precisely in those areas where we are least prepared to admit a need for development.

How we manage this transition to an environment that allows development needs to be championed, owned and therefore acted upon constructively is one of the major challenges facing all organizations today. There are a number of important steps that should be taken which will help shift organizational thinking in this direction:

ACTION STEPS

Go back to basics in training

There used to be an old maxim that the best way of learning the job was doing it. We ignore the sense of this at our cost. The closer we can get necessary training to the place of work and the work routines of individuals the better chance we have of establishing the new system, behaviour, skill, etc., as an essential part of their work patterns.

Establishing an action-learning test to set against all training propositions you come across would help. Just ask if there is opportunity to observe/understand; discuss/review; practise; gain feedback/review; improve understanding further and then, if necessary practise again. The closer the practice is to reality the more success is likely to be achieved.

Reduce training programmes and increase learning opportunities

A training course, particularly for any sort of management skill/ behaviour/process, should be the last resort. There are literally tens and tens of development opportunities that allow people to learn from experience and to practise new skills in a relatively risk-free environment. A quick list:

- Project assignment in a new field
- Role swap
- Appointment to a management committee/group/task force
- Appointment as a school governor
- Presentation to senior management/visitors
- Given responsibility for a new starter
- Involvement in a professional body
- Manage an organizational change
- Assignment to another function
- Organize a conference/convention

All of these should be accompanied by:

- A clear agreement as to why the activity is being undertaken
- A setting of some goals relating to personal development and goals for successful achievement of the business objectives associated with the activity.

If so then they are likely to be far more effective than any internal or external programme that addresses issues in an organizational vacuum.

Move from control to empowerment

None of these activities stands an earthly of making any real impression unless we review our business systems and processes. Much of what this move to learning is all about is transferring the initiative to the individual. By doing this we are giving them responsibility for their own development. By letting them take responsibility for themselves we give them far greater motivation to address their learning priorities. We can destroy this, or at the very least seriously damage it, by continuing to operate systems that are in themselves barriers to taking responsibility for oneself. The key systems are the financial ones and those normally found supporting the HR function.

Expense procedures that give no room for responsible personal judgement; expenditure approval systems with ridiculously low sign-off levels; authority approval processes that take weeks and involve everyone in the hierarchy. None of these empowers people. They all impose controls. I have worked with very few finance functions that see their role as supporting the business: most expound a doctrine of policing that Stalin would have been proud of. And few HR functions have much to be proud of, with their inflexible policy manuals, closed development systems which give no feedback to the individuals they are supposed to develop, appraisal systems which are as threatening as the annual school report and remuneration systems that give no flexibility or choice. What chance the encouragement of self-development?

Role-model the commitment

This is probably the most difficult, but the most important. Unless those who work for you and with you believe that they can admit to their needs and gain support and commitment to their action plans then all of the above may have been in vain. The most successful way of providing an organizational support network is to look at mentoring. Most of us at some points in our careers have had a mentor – some of us maybe more than one. For nearly all this will have been an informal relationship struck up with a more senior manager normally only indirectly associated with our day-to-day role. For most it was a positive influence. We listened and learned from their experience. Introducing a more formal acknowledgement of this process, providing support for it and giving people permission to seek advice/mentoring from others outside their line enhances the move from control to empowerment and opens up a rich seam of learning potential.

STOCKTAKE 6: LEARNING TO LEARN

This stocktake gets you to think about your own development needs in the context of the actions discussed above. Having thought about yourself and formulated some action plans, you should then look at learning opportunities and the development of those who work for you.

■ Start by reminding yourself of the development needs that you identified in the last stocktake

1	5
2	6
3	7
4	8

■ Taking each need separately, identify three options that you believe could help you to improve your knowledge/skill ability. Be as creative/lateral as you like at this stage.

Development need	Option 1	Option 2	Option 3
1			
2			
3			
4			
5			
6			
7			
8			

■ Now decide upon two options you could put into effect now without reference to anyone else. Which ones are you going to commit to and what goals/timescales are you going to contract with yourself to achieve?

Option	Goal	Time scale
1		
2		

■ Now consider which options you will need to contract with your line manager/supervisor to achieve. Select two. What contract will you make?

Option	Goal	Time scale
1		
2		

■ And finally ...

> 1 Have you got a mentor? If not why not think of one or two people whom you would like as a mentor? Why not agree with your line manager to approach them to see if they would help?
>
> 2 What can you do for those that work for and/or with you to help them develop their own approach to learning?
>
> 3 What can you do to promote the discussion on the systems and the role modelling required to turn development activity into something that genuinely adds value to your business?

THE CHALLENGE OF CAREER DEVELOPMENT – TAKING CHARGE OF YOUR OWN FUTURE

The final piece of the jigsaw that makes up the development picture is career development. If we empower people in their current roles then we must give them responsibility for their own careers. This is where the learning challenge and the demographic challenge neatly come together.

Demographics may point to skill shortages in key areas but they also point to the phenomena of the mid-twentieth century, the baby boomers, staying put at the top of many corporate trees for some time to come. The cause of this very real problem can be seen in the economic woes of most Western economies in the 1980s and early 1990s. These, along with the severe restructuring that much of the UK's industry adopted from the mid-1970s onwards, as technology advanced and energy and other raw material costs spiralled, have meant a major reduction in the number of management roles as well as industrial and administrative roles. Flatter structures, fewer roles, more 40–50 year olds at the top rather than 50–60 year olds, mean that whilst opportunities abound at entry level for the post-baby boomers of the 1990s they get scarcer and scarcer for those further up.

This means that for many of us a redefinition of career development is required. This redefinition will have to be lateral rather than vertical. We will need to look for opportunity in new roles, new functions, new businesses. All will require new skills. These will only be acquired successfully through learning from experience – most likely from others. Career development will come to mean the continuous acquisition of skills and experience from a wide range of roles throughout one's working life. Progression through organizational structures will have to come to mean less and variety and challenge will come from greater horizontal leaps.

We could well end up comfortable with the notion of two or three entirely separate careers within one working lifetime. The only way we will successfully manage this challenge is by making the transition to learning as an organizational philosophy and management process. This is one of the few options open to businesses from the EC and North America that will allow them to compete successfully with businesses from economies which do not face the particular dilemmas surrounding access to skills and declining populations. Developing learning organizations, they will be well prepared for anything as their ability to adapt quickly, learning lessons from new experiences, will be well established.

4 Moving from control to commitment: structures and styles in organizations

The traditional image of an organizational pyramid and of management being the task of controlling ever increasing numbers of people is redundant. Yet, perversely, we continue to prolong its influence by persisting with the systems and styles of management devised to support it. Much of our industry still designs structures that ignore changes in technology, new skill sets, communication developments and the sheer pace and extent of change that these, and other more economic pressures, impose on today's organizations. We need to anticipate the shape of the future organization and start developing the skills required to succeed within it.

On most public and in-house training courses we continue to provide skills development in those areas associated with managing large groups of people as a controller of activity. How many of us have gone through 'Tell, Sell' sessions or practised situational leadership skills, appraisal skills, objective setting skills and, horror of horrors, job design and evaluation briefings. Unless they are very enlightened these spring from a fundamental assumption that you the manager need these skills to manage subordinates.

As we change structures in the workplace these skills have less and less utility. In fact they are likely to generate significant dysfunctional behaviour unless they are adapted. The potential for damaging internal pain as organizations change to meet the challenge of the 1990s is considerable. How we develop organizations and the assessment and development of new skill sets to work effectively in them will be a major determinant, therefore, of business success.

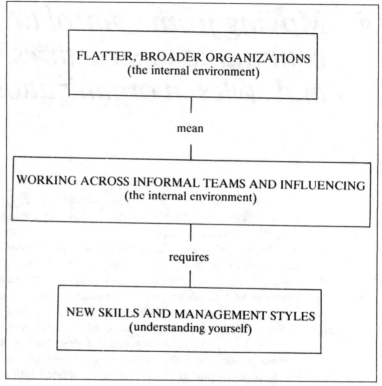

Figure 4.1 Structures and styles in organizations

THE FALL OF THE LINE AND THE RISE OF THE NETWORK

In this case network refers neither to your local TV station nor to your office computer link-up: rather to an organizational state of mind. Abuse has it that advertising, media and public relations types do nothing but 'network' and as such the word has fallen into disrepute. The relentless PR executive always ready with their card to pounce on a potentially lucrative contact has become one of the images of the 'Yuppie'-dominated 1980s. Before we dismiss the concept out of hand, however, we should remember the principle upon which it is based: influence through good relationships and access through personal knowledge are crucial to success when you are relying on others to make decisions that affect your own business fortunes.

BACKGROUND

Consider then this principle when faced with the organizations in which many of us still operate. Most of today's organizations have their roots in the principles of 'scientific management' which gained credence in the early twentieth century. This system, developed by Taylor and Sloan, was based fundamentally on a 'command and control' model of company management that first introduced the concepts of line and staff management, management layers and structures and the need for documented and controlled policies and procedures.

What was essential to the successful operation of this type of organization was stability. The major assumption behind these high-control cultures was that little would change the demographic, technical or market conditions that applied at the time. There was a plentiful supply of unskilled or semi-skilled workers who needed little training to work simple machinery.

What the 'control' organization did was establish a clear process for the delivery of goods to meet a constant market demand. Decision-making was the prerogative of the senior managers, intermediate layers of management transmitted these decisions and developed detailed implementation plans which were then actioned by first-line supervision and the semi- and unskilled workforce. These processes were held together by a series of clearly defined and very restrictive policies and procedures outside of which it was impossible to operate unless agreed by the senior management.

Obviously these structures dictated a need for specific skills which managers had to acquire in order to succeed at the different levels within the organization. These skills centred on the ability to direct and control the work of large numbers of people, e.g. clerks, craftsmen, machine operators, etc. They demanded obedience to the edicts of the hierarchy and respect for the authority of the position of a senior. The position and placing of jobs within such structures became a very important part of the controlling process. Knowledge became a key to control. It became more limited the further down the organization a manager was. Job Evaluation and Need to Know briefings are the direct offspring of these 'control' structures, forming substantial parts of their policy and procedure.

In the early 1960s two significant changes started to undermine the foundations of these types of organizations: the gradual removal of trade tariffs following the second world war and the development of electronic storage and manipulation of data. The increasing internationalization of competition, and for the UK the impact of far more productive and market-led foreign competition, placed significant economic pressures on organizations struggling to stay profitable. The impact of electronic storage of data was primarily in the ability it gave lower levels of management to make decisions and to take power previously held by their superiors through exclusive access to knowledge.

Information solutions interestingly were initially seen as coming through cumbersome mainframe processes, with organizations using them to control even more from the centre. Driven by finance functions which epitomized the control cultures, the information technology of the 1970s and early 1980s focused on providing information upwards to a limited few who would then use it to make key decisions. Systems departments were normally part of finance empires peopled by specialists through whom access was gained to information. On-line access and enquiry was virtually unheard of.

The organizational impact of economic decline and low productivity over a twenty-year period hit earlier than that of user-orientated technology. The recession of the early 1980s forced many concerns to consider their organization structures primarily in terms of a clear association between 'heads' and the largest single cost in their profit and loss accounts. For example in their study of culture and its impact on performance Kotter and Heskett cite the changes brought about by Sir John Harvey Jones in his drive to create a high-performing business from a rather moribund and increasingly less profitable organization.[1] His restructuring reduced corporate headquarters from 1,200 to 400 and the overall workforce from 74,700 in 1981 to 56,230 in 1987: a drop of 25 per cent. ICI were not alone. The 1980s saw massive shake-outs in manufacturing and associated industries, with significant reductions in labour and considerable rises in productivity.

These shake-outs and the consequent improvements in productivity were made possible by two major changes to the way the work itself was carried out. First, some of the unskilled and semi-skilled workforce upgraded their skills. Better technology and increased mechanization forced employers to train those who were willing or had some of the basic skills to perform advanced technical roles. Those already skilled acquired additional skills. This allowed major reductions in manpower levels with significant savings in the costs of production. The second change was in the structures and systems of management which were developed to supervise the new work groups. Significant de-layering of management structures took place. Much flatter organizations require less bureaucracy, and the revolution in information technology that turned the individual rather than the organization into the prime customer gave companies the flexibility they needed to reduce the levels of clerical and administrative support that had characterized many offices.

TENSIONS

What had happened therefore in manufacturing industries in the 1980s – and is happening to service industries in the 1990s – was the jettisoning of the traditional organization. Managers and staff were empowered by technology, by being given greater skills and responsibilities, and by having more operating 'room' around them to take control for themselves and to become more independent. Quite often these moves were reinforced by a process of decentralization to regions/divisions or profit centres which aimed to push responsibility down through the organization. With this development have come some major tensions.

Process no longer fits the structure

What we have created is a very different type of organization, supported by and reliant on the transmission and dissemination of electronically stored data. But this 'datocracy' is being hampered in its effectiveness by our stubborn persistence in not recognizing its inherent characteristic: there are very few line managers. Flat organizations, decentralized decision-making and powerful information technology drive a very different form of management process. Data and its speed of delivery (and therefore the required speed of response) impose an imperative to do the right thing quickly: the cumbersome discussion process which is still characteristic of many major companies impedes progress and takes the decision away from those who are best informed and placed to make it.

Knowledge no longer equates with power

Breadth of responsibility replaces depth of expertise the nearer one gets to managing board level. Going to the 'boss' for expert advice is no longer adequate. For many managers the issues that require decisions are ones where bosses are ill-equipped themselves to make a judgement: the practice of retaining knowledge and power in a single senior manager is a serious threat to reaching the right decision at the right time.

Change can no longer be imposed

The implementation of key decisions becomes extremely important in these new organizations, particularly when they involve major change: the old-style process of a small group of senior managers developing a total 'solution' can no longer be seen as valid. Better informed and better skilled, many employees have already grabbed responsibility and will expect change to grant them more.

The answer, unsurprisingly, comes back to networks. What we have created are structures that require us to change our management processes from those espoused in scientific management and refined over the last sixty years or so to those that underpin rather than undercut our decentralized datocracies. We require orientation so that we understand that we are managing in a real matrix where we are going to rely on many others who do not work for us, or even with us. Yet the decisions of these people will have a major impact on our ability to succeed in our business. They (and we) need to know this, recognize it and, where appropriate, ensure that they have mechanisms for including us in any decision-making that affects us: and vice versa. Stocktake 7 provides for determining your own matrix.

ACTION STEPS

Speed up decision-making

So, for decision-making to be timely, it has to be carried out at the lowest possible level with a clear understanding that more senior levels are not there to second-guess those they have entrusted with the running of local units. This requires the establishment of co-ordinating mechanisms that give clear guidance as to what is decided where and a speedy method of testing that an ambiguous issue has been best resolved. Whether organized in divisions or geographical regions or strategic business units, for most businesses in the 1990s this will mean the senior team deals with little else than setting and directing strategy and reviewing decisions that have a major impact on that strategy, such as acquisitions, disposals, significant capital expenditure proposals and stakeholder relations. It will mean that the management systems and processes currently held centrally such as job grading, salaries, new product development, marketing campaigns, sales promotions, bonus schemes, etc., will have to be handed to those best able to take the right decisions for the market/business/organization they are managing.

Develop centres of expertise

What this entails for the business is a requirement to ensure that the best possible 'specialist' advice is available to each decision-making unit through the establishment of influential and respected functions which cover areas such as finance, human resources, legal matters, public relations, marketing, etc. The roles of these functions will not be to police activity – this is what often happens and is merely the continuation of a control culture by more (or less!) subtle means – but through good consulting skills to provide support to each unit so it reaches its business goal. Support does not mean acquiescence, essentially it requires partnership.

Involve people in decisions that affect their work

As responsibility cascades down through structures it creates an expectation: that of involvement. By this I do not mean employee involvement schemes such as those espoused by unions or by some of the EC's major economies. Rather a much more immediate and far more rewarding form of involvement: participating in the shaping of change. I choose my words carefully: not participating in the development or directing of change, rather the shaping of it. It is still clearly the responsibility of senior management to set direction and to challenge the organization constantly to ensure that it continues to travel in the right direction. Much of the change that will happen in an organization will come out of this. The most effective change, however, is that which is owned and implemented at the level at which it is aimed. This requires us to have the courage to share broad strategic aims with key employees whose roles will be directly affected and let them devise the detail of how best to achieve what is required. After all, if it is your solution you tend to try much harder to ensure it succeeds.

STOCKTAKE 7: MAPPING A MATRIX, DEVELOPING A NETWORK

As a manager it is essential to be clear on what roles either directly or indirectly impact on your own responsibilities and effectiveness. This stocktake encourages you to draw up your own matrix for your general responsibilities. Remember – for a particular project or responsibility your matrix is very likely to change.

■ List your major areas of responsibility. For each of these write down the names/job roles of those people with whom you are expected to liaise/consult before taking a major decision. Indicate in brackets whether they are a junior, peer or senior and whether they are directly in your line (up or down) or indirectly. By functions I mean finance, marketing, production, etc., and I would suggest putting contacts in your own function into the 'other teams' column.

Area of responsibility	Own team	Other teams	Other functions	Other divisions
1				
2				
3				
4				

5

6

7

8

9

10

■ Do a count of

1 Direct line mentions
2 Indirect line mentions
3 Juniors
4 Peers
5 Subordinates

■ What did this tell you?

■ Now, repeat the same matrix but instead of noting those
you are required to liaise with/consult, list those with
whom you believe you are on 'networking' terms, e.g.
friends, regular contacts, etc., where you feel you have
some influence or support. Again in brackets note
whether direct or indirect, and whether junior senior or
peer.

	Area of responsibility	Own team	Other teams	Other functions	Other divisions
1					
2					
3					
4					
5					
6					
7					
8					
9					
10					

■ Do a count of

1 Direct line mentions
2 Indirect line mentions
3 Juniors

4   Peers
5   Subordinates

■   What did this tell you?

1
2
3
4
5
etc.

■   Looking at your matrix, where did your network match
    your matrix?

1
2
3
4
5
etc.

■   Where did your network fail to match your matrix?

1
2
3
4
5
etc.

■   Take each area where you failed either substantially or
    wholly to match your network to your matrix and set
    yourself an action plan to improve your effectiveness

    Area   *Action plan*

1
2
3
4
5
etc.

> ■   After six months do this again and notice what has
> changed. The key question is then to review your
> activities in the areas for improvement and to see
> whether your effectiveness has changed!

CHANGING THE HOW AS WELL AS THE WHAT

In order to succeed in the organization of the 1990s managers are
going to have to think very differently about how they approach
the task of management. If management is no longer about
control, but about gaining commitment through the empowerment
of others, then what is required is genuine leadership. As part of
our need to develop a greater understanding of ourselves and our
own effectiveness we need to understand our effect on others.
Appreciating the range of management styles that are open to us
and developing the appropriate skills will not only ensure personal
success but will also build success for the business or organization.

Networks, co-ordination, matrices, decentralization and delegation of responsibility call for skills very different from those we
have been used to acquiring and exercising. Many of our favourite
role models, our current bosses and our peers all exhibit behaviours as managers which were well suited to the control mentality
but sit uneasily with the way in which we need to work if we are to
maximize our business effectiveness.

If your organization has a training department or offers courses,
either internal or external, just spend a few minutes reviewing the
subject areas. How many are dedicated to skills related to the
control of people or resources? At a guess the majority, if not a
substantial majority. So what is needed? A complete rethink of the
management skills base would go a long way. My key suggestions
for change are:

ACTION STEPS

Feedback and coaching rather than criticism and judgement

Empowerment means very little as a phrase. You only genuinely
empower others if you can transfer skills successfully, using

effective feedback, employing clear examples of positive and less positive behaviour to reinforce understanding, and then coach. This is true for personal and technical skills: if you ever catch yourself saying, 'I don't know how many times I've told you ...' ask yourself if you ever once stopped to demonstrate, agreed clear standards and supported learning through the discussion of successes as well as failures. Asking the basic question 'Why was this time different?' is a powerful learning tool.

Influencing to facilitate understanding rather than imposing solutions

Leadership is not having the answer to everything and direction can be given in other ways than by you making the final decision in every case. Developing a more facilitative style of management is a very powerful tool in a business. First, it creates the confidence in those you are dealing with that you respect their ideas and point of view; second, it is a far less directive way of making your point – let the answers people give to your questions become your most telling arguments. Since you will increasingly rely on others to accede to your proposals rather than impose your decisions, they have to be convinced that your ideas meet their own needs as well as yours. The ability to influence becomes vastly more important the more distant your matrix is from your direct line relationships.

Risking the impact of innovation rather than stay with the safe

Creativity can liberate organizations. We have to begin to establish management styles that welcome and encourage the innovative and that support the taking of risk. A key part of this is to set up learning processes which review the implementation and results of innovation, and, where failure occurs, ensure key points are understood and that the organization as a whole benefits from the experience. Whether we do this through 'Groups of Ten' processes where individuals are put into groups and encouraged to come up with ten ideas to develop their business or improve their effectiveness, or through creativity budgets where staff are given small budgets with which to pursue ideas and the support of R&D functions should these show promise, we need to meet this challenge.

Initiating and managing rather than protecting and preserving territory

In a strategic review of a business in which I participated we issued a challenge to the senior team: think of key changes we could make in your own and other functions that would improve our efficiency and reduce our long-term cost base. Not particularly original but an effective process nonetheless. Unsurprisingly, they were full of ideas for their colleagues but remained silent, for the most part, bar some cosmetics, on their own area. Change is a threat – it is a threat to the *status quo* – however, it need not be a personal threat if it is seen as a constant opportunity. We have to have the courage to be in the vanguard of change in our businesses. If we do, then we will be well placed to meet the challenges of a fast-moving business environment and the pressure for constant performance improvement.

STOCKTAKE 8: TRANSFORMING MANAGEMENT INTO LEADERSHIP

In Stocktake 5 you established your key strengths and weaknesses and developed an action plan. Even if we have the skills, or plans in hand to acquire them, we can still find considerable difficulty in the application of these skills as we find ourselves without the supporting management processes. This stocktake aims to help you establish some internal processes for yourself which should reinforce and develop four of the skills discussed above.

Feedback and coaching

■ Take your last appraisal (verbal and written if possible) and any other pieces of feedback your boss has given you over the past six to twelve months. List here all the comments that were critical of your performance. Sort them into 'positive and negative'.

Positive	*Negative*
1	
2	
3	

4
5
etc.

■ What characteristics did the positive criticisms have in common?

1
2
3
4
5
etc.

■ What characteristics did the negative criticisms have in common?

1
2
3
4
5
etc.

■ What areas were missed out altogether where you wished for feedback?

1
2
3
4
5
etc.

■ Is there any one (or two at a maximum) area where you believe you require coaching from your boss or another individual in the organization in order to improve your performance?

Using the data above, plan a feedback session for your boss, using the following structure

■ Things I would like you to continue doing, as they are
motivational and positive, although pointing out areas
where I could improve

1
2
3
4
5
etc.

■ Things I would like you to stop doing, as they
demotivate me and do nothing to encourage me to
improve

1
2
3
4
5
etc.

■ Things I would like you to consider doing because I
know they would motivate me and encourage me to
improve

1
2
3
4
5
etc.

As an example of this latter category: 'I would like to
book some time for you to help coach me with ... (your
pet need). My objectives for this session would be ...
(your goals).'

■ Have you any feedback for me (a) about this process (b)
about things I could stop/start/continue that would
improve my performance?

1
2
3
4
5
etc.

■ Following this imaginary encounter, now book an
appointment, explain what you would like to do before
you arrive and note below

1   Your feelings on completion

2   Your successes

3   Your failures and what you would do differently next
time

4   Your follow-up action plan

Listening and questioning

Think of your next major meeting/discussion where you
have clear views and a preferred solution.

■ What is the background?

1
2
3
4
5
etc.

■ What is your solution?

1
2
3
4
5
etc.

■ Who do you need to persuade?

1
2
3
4
5
etc.

■ For each key player see if you can identify their preferred option, what their major objection would be to accepting yours and what yours offers to meet their needs.

Key player   Their option   Their problem   Your solution

1
2
3
4
5
etc.

■ Now design a series of questions that are aimed at each key player and which allow them to provide pointers towards your solution. Think of three for each person.

Person   Question 1   Question 2   Question 3

1
2
3

4
5
etc.

■ Following the meeting, review your effectiveness

1   Your successes

2   Your failures and what you would do differently next
    time

3   Your follow-up action plan

    Gain feedback from others at the meeting. Did they
    notice anything different? Were you more or less
    effective as an influencer? Can you interest them in
    working on these skill areas with you?

5 Ethics, the environment and organizational effectiveness

As we now face the twenty-first century there has been a major shift in public views and expectations of organizations – not only those in the private sector but also those with public-sector roles and responsibilities. Increasingly we are being judged as much by our environmental and ethical standards as by our products and profits and/or efficiency. If the *Exxon Valdiz*, Chernobyl, Bhopal, ozone depletion and the retreat of the rain forests were the environmental disasters of the 1980s then Guinness, Boesky, Maxwell, Blue Arrow, BCCI, Salamon Brothers and the Recruit scandal (to name but a few) were the ethical equivalent. All of them as the decade progressed had an increasing impact on the standing of business in public opinion.

These shifts in opinion are not just swelling the ranks of pressure groups or affecting smaller investors. Major institutional investors with sufficient funds to make a difference, institutions such as schools and universities which influence the future work-force, television, radio and newspaper journalists whose articles help form opinion, trade unions and increasing numbers of politicians from the right as well as the left are all now demanding tighter environmental standards and the establishment of clear ethical codes across both private and public sectors. This shift in public attitudes will need a clearly thought out response from business and public-sector organizations and requires us as managers to consider the whole range of policies and activities for which we are responsible to ensure that they are in line with the attitudes and opinions of our customers and our employees – both current and future.

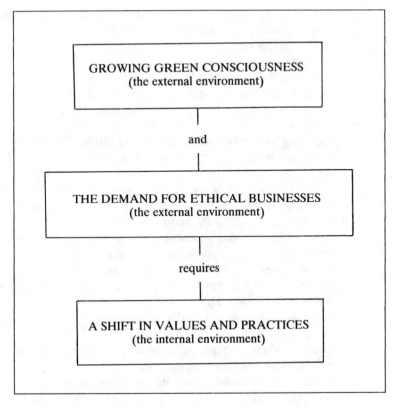

Figure 5.1 The impact of ethical and environmental pressure on organizations

GOING GREEN

In 1990 a report to the UK's Institute of Personnel Management caused a major stir in the columns of most of the British press. The *Financial Times* headline ran: 'Warning over shift in job values'.[1] International survey research had discerned a clear shift in employee attitudes over the last ten years. These covered a range of issues such as the increasing importance of performance-related pay and the impact of increasing environmental awareness. The key point in this respect was that over 30 per cent of 18–24 year olds wanted to find work which did not damage society and was socially useful. The conclusions for companies whose products were seen as damaging and socially unattractive were unambiguous: increasing recruitment and retention problems and the very real potential of more restrictive regulation. This on top of the more obvious impact on demand for their products.

Before those of us who do not work in chemical, food production or tobacco companies start to feel smug we should just pause for a while to think of the consequences for our own businesses. As so-called 'dirty' industries start to suffer from the impact of the environment and health lobbies so two things will happen. For those like the chemical and food sectors which supply other industries the increase in their costs will inevitably mean that others' will rise. After a while these increases will squeeze margins so much that they will have to be passed on to consumers, putting increased pressure on the economy.

In addition those industries which become less attractive as employers to key groups in society will inevitably act in two areas: recruit among target groups not yet in the employment market and increase the entry point salaries in their traditional recruiting group of 18–24 year olds. These two actions will only worsen the impact of the demographic shift discussed earlier in the book. The costs of employment will rise for all of us, particularly in areas of skill shortage where younger employees are important such as information technology and engineering.

All of us have the opportunity to alleviate the impact of these pressures by reviewing where we stand in relation to the increasingly green mind set of both consumers and potential and current employees. We are all aware of the impact of a whole range of environmental issues and indeed of the well publicized responses by businesses as well as governments to them. Whilst the focus on CFCs, tropical hardwoods and carbon dioxide and sulphur dioxide emissions has held the headlines many people have seen these as global issues which can only be addressed by governments and industry leaders. However, environmental policies are not just the prerogative of the great and the good. As managers we can set environmental standards for our own areas of responsibility. These standards need not require significant allocations of scarce resources and may, in many instances, reduce the costs of operations.

It is also fair to say that it is at the operating level that so many high-minded declarations of company policy are seriously undermined. How often have we come across individuals within organizations with very public commitments to improving the environment who completely contradict that commitment? My favourite story concerning this is of the advert run by an organization I worked for in the mid-1980s showing a fox in countryside just outside one of their plants. The text extolled the company's virtues as an environmentally friendly manufacturing giant. When I was posted to the plant I mentioned this advert to a number of people, all of whom gave me the same answer: they found the fox dead outside the gate and stuffed it!

I am sure that in reality they did no such thing, but there was enough evidence around the site that undercut the public pronouncements to engender a considerable level of cynicism. That cynicism had little to do with the company's senior management – although they were certainly setting standards that could only be aspirational for plants that in some cases were over thirty years old. Rather it was clearly the consequence of local managers making local decisions. We can all have an impact, therefore, as most managers have some degree of control over the what, where and how operations are carried out. As environmental issues become more and more important there are three key areas which we should consider:

ACTION STEPS

Energy consumption

The biggest contribution we can make to reducing the 'greenhouse' effect and the incidence of 'acid rain' is to reduce the energy our operations consume. By doing so we also have a positive impact on what for many of us is the biggest single budget item after staff costs. Despite this being the most obvious area to look for opportunities, far too few organizations really explore the possibilities – most stick to printed exhortations to turn off the lights! Why? One of the biggest reasons is that schemes which allow substantial savings in energy consumption tend to involve capital expenditure. Although the payback periods can be very attractive, when resources are tight energy saving will always come second to new plant, equipment and premises if they are essential to the continuing success of the organization.

However, as environmental awareness becomes more and more important to success the relevance of the schemes and the opportunity cost of not implementing them will become increasingly obvious. Simple things like sensors in washrooms for both lights and flush mechanisms and replacing bulbs with the lower wattage 'low energy' variety can generate significant savings and underpin environmental commitment. Inefficient air conditioning and heating systems can be wasteful and add more carbon dioxide to the atmosphere. Air conditioning which is replaced can mean the release of CFCs into the atmosphere unless we ensure it is done safely.

Resource management

This has two main thrusts: ensuring that wherever possible resources are recycled effectively and also that materials employed in the organization have minimal or no negative impact on the environment.

Recylcing is considerably more complicated than it initially sounds. Recycled paper is fine for photocopies and post-it notes (yes, there are recycled ones) and for brown envelopes, inter-office envelopes, etc. It is not so good for formal letter paper and envelopes. By the time it is bleached the positive of recycling the resource is completely outweighed by the amounts of energy (and bleach) employed to achieve the finish required. The answer is 'forest farmed' paper from renewable woodlands – but it does take a lot of digging to arrive at this answer. There are not just cost opportunities where the basic grade paper can be utilized (e.g. notepads, etc.) but also income opportunities from contracting to collect all your waste paper for a recycling company and selling to them by the 'skip'.

Paper is the obvious recycling candidate, but glass, aluminium, textiles, vegetable waste from canteens, etc., can all find a good home.

Auditing the resources and materials you employ in an organization is also a challenge. You may discover that the standard electrical fire extinguisher contains a gas just as damaging to the ozone layer as CFCs. Up till now, however, it has not been possible to replace it with something as effective but less harmful. Having said that, it is possible for example to ensure cleaning materials are sensitive, waste bins have paper rather than plastic sacs, the kitchens serve nothing in polystyrene and pencils are wood rather than plastic. Office furniture should not be of tropical hardwood (goodbye to your dream of the mahogany desk and matching meeting table) and your drinks machine should serve waxed-paper rather than plastic cups. Better still if you put your favourite unhygienic but environmentally sound chipped china mug under the spout.

Office and administrative processes

Administrative procedures have an environmental impact: in the age of the disc the day file is an expensive and redundant append-age. Pinning circulation lists to some documents rather than copying for circulation will not slow progress down. Double-sided photocopying should become the 'norm' – new machines make it easy. There are literally as many opportunities as there are current processes.

The biggest challenge for those of us in large organizations is to reduce intra-organization memos: often redundant, mainly intended to give the impression of activity, or to protect one's position, rarely adding real value, they are the scourge of most managers. The problem can be attacked by setting standards on the virtue of direct face-to-face communication, pulling people up for notes that are protecting themselves or others, etc., but it will not be effectively addressed until organizations switch to, and utilize to the full, electronic mail systems.

CHANGING THOSE WITH WHOM YOU HAVE INFLUENCE

In many respects other organizations with which we interact can be influenced to follow a good example. At one end are contractors and suppliers, part of whose contracts, you can insist, refers to environmental best practice. Those whom you supply can be per-suaded if you can show it is in their interest – particularly if cost saving is a real benefit.

The most positive impact will be with the consumer – and as more and more boards of directors cast about for examples of how their organizations respect the environment owing to consumer/ shareholder demands, being in a position to demonstrate actions rather than intentions will be very important. Influence in this respect will come from showing responsiveness to consumer and employee attitudes and aspirations – by establishing your own area as an example of best practice and keeping abreast of the burgeoning literature in what will be the biggest growth area of management practice over the next five years.

STOCKTAKE 9: ENVIRONMENTAL AUDIT

■ Consider your own area of responsibility. What do you use of the following?

1 Light
2 Heat
3 Air conditioning
4 Electronic equipment

Against each of these areas put at least one action that you could take without having to refer to anyone else and which would reduce your energy consumption.

■ Now put at least one action against each of these which will need others' co-operation and/or approval which you believe you could argue for effectively.

Action list	*Contact*
1	
2	
3	
4	

■ Now think about the resources and materials that you employ. List the top fifteen as far as you can in order of magnitude. Then check for recycling possibilities and for the possibility of substituting a more environmentally friendly alternative

Resource/ Material	*Recycling option*	*Alternative option*
1		

2

3

4

5

6

7

8

9

10

11

12

13

14

15

■ Now review the office/administrative processes you
employ in your area of responsibility. Start first with
those you have control over. Against each one put an
action that could reduce the energy, materials,
resources, etc., currently needed.

Process   *Possible actions*

1

2

3

4

5

etc.

■ Now consider those which are imposed by the organization you work for. Which ones do you think are areas where with some good arguments you may find support for change?

Process	Possible actions
1	
2	
3	
4	
5	
etc.	

■ Finally list here the organizations (inside and outside work) with which you have sufficient influence to be able to persuade them to follow your example and take on the challenge of making their own organizations environmentally aware.

Organization	Possible changes	Success measure
1		
2		
3		
4		
5		
etc.		

Beside each one put a success measure: what one thing would you really like to see them do? Come back to this in six to nine months' time and do a check. How successful were you and, if you failed, why?

ETHICS AND THE ORGANIZATION

There is one very obvious difference between the early 1980s and the early 1990s as we review the really significant issues for the next decade. It has to be the fundamental shift in commercial thinking that now believes there is considerable value in ensuring that the public perception of the organization reflects honesty, fair dealing and a sense of responsibility to customers and the wider community. This shift I believe springs directly from the public disquiet in the late 1980s and reinforced by more recent scandals such as the BCCI affair. The more far-sighted organizations saw that unless their public reputation was protected their long-term profitability was at risk. A survey of consumers published in 1992 in the UK indicated that 79 per cent considered an organization's reputation important in guiding purchasing decisions.[2]

It is clear that business in particular – but increasingly this is important for public-sector organizations – cannot afford to be casual about their reputation in the marketplace. This is, however, not just an argument for spending more on a good PR firm, although the survey certainly detected more of the marketing budget being spent on this than on classic promotions and advertising. Slick PR is always exposed in the end. Organizations will need to review the whole range of operating values and processes which they employ and establish a clear set of ethical principles. Only when customers, consumers, suppliers and employees can see these principles at work in the day-to-day operations will they be convinced of a sound ethical approach to the way business is conducted.

This all sounds good stuff; few are likely to disagree. When it comes to considering implementation it can become a nightmare. Consider what is meant by ethics: at one extreme we are talking about a rigid set of principles which set a moral code of behaviour and at the other we are talking about ensuring that you avoid the fate of those connected with the illegal share support operations of the 1980s – remember, they said they didn't think they were acting illegally. There is no clear definition: the Oxford Dictionary offers several, from moral principles to rules of conduct. The essential point is that, however you define ethical principles, they have to ensure that what you do fits in with the overall position of the organization on whose behalf you are acting.

This means that managers will need to develop operating guidelines that allow those who work with and for them to understand clearly what is expected of them and how they should conduct themselves whilst representing the organization. In doing this we should consider the following:

ACTION STEPS

Set and communicate high standards

This may seem obvious, but I believe it is the one area that is neglected over any other. Of the three divisions I worked for at GrandMet, and the two at Shell, only one regularly published the standards it set in respect of dealings with contractors, suppliers, customers and the giving and taking of hospitality, gifts, etc. I am sure all the others held pretty similar views and had at one time or another published a policy which then sat in a manual on a shelf. However, if I had walked round and asked people what the standard was, for say Christmas gifts, I am sure I would have received many different answers. In these cases what we were really relying on was individual standards set without reference to a greater corporate good.

It is not just the setting and communicating that is important. The other area is to ensure they are reinforced at key moments. For example, with constant pressure to reduce budgets and costs and to produce the best sales figures in a challenging market many people who are basically honest will consider taking short cuts because it is expedient to do so. These could range from dubious selling into the trade to meet sales targets at year end to outright bribery and corruption to secure contracts. Many people will not realize that, although at the other end of the scale from the obviously illegal, making arrangements say to be charged less for one contract on the basis of assuring the next is wrong. It is meeting the company target, they may argue, and this is what they get paid for. Setting challenging targets and pushing people to achieve them is one thing; doing so without ensuring there is an ethical framework in which efforts can legitimately take place is as much an immoral act as the bribery resorted to by the employee to achieve a goal.

Review key policies and processes

Frequently there are considerable gaps between the policies espoused by an organization and practice on the ground. Publishing a set of ethical principles and then undercutting them by knowingly or unwittingly endorsing actions that do not fit with them can only encourage employees to treat them with a large degree of cynicism.

A classic example is how the organization manages its own corporate entertaining and activity programme. Careful scrutiny will often reveal the same people attending all the events regardless of whether there is a legitimate business interest in their being there. This gets perceived in the business as a gravy train and one that is restricted to the top few managers. Employees become disillusioned and start asking why they can't enjoy such events – when the opportunity comes along they will jump at it without any reference to your well written principles that call for consideration of the consequences. This can be avoided on the whole by thinking first about the level and amount of gifting, hospitality, etc., that your organization carries out and second by providing access to these events and/or facilities for ordinary employees. Running an efficiency challenge and then ensuring the best team goes to the football or the races along with the customers they serve would make a good example. Good for the team, good for the customers and good for the business.

Other areas that will need review are purchasing policies, donations to political parties and pressure groups, investment policies and the like. They all have consequences for a robust ethical approach to business. One area often ignored, especially by larger organizations, is the ethics of paying bills – particularly to small suppliers. This is just as much a reflection of your approach to business as any other and can have very damaging consequences for reputation and longer-term business prosperity. If there are terms of business which you have accepted, then stick to them. Meeting the company's cash flow targets is a legitimate process. In doing so send out a note asking managers not to agree to payments until date X if they are making agreements say at the end of the trading year. That is a legitimate and ethical way of meeting all parties' needs. Withholding much-needed cash having agreed to pay it is unethical, poor practice and in the long term loses you customers and consumers.

Redefine the role of audit

As part of the role of the audit function managers should consider widening the brief to cover not just the obvious areas such as expense claim fraud but also the wider ethical principles in the area of current policy and practice – very much in the manner of the environmental audit that you constructed for your own area earlier in the chapter.

And finally the personal challenge . . .

As in so much of management one of the most powerful ways to generate strong ethical principles amongst those who work with and for you is to be a positive role model. Checking yourself and the standards you choose to operate by before setting out to get others to stick to them has to be the very first stage of any programme designed to establish ethical business practice.

Given all this, it may seem difficult to 'go it alone' just for your own area of responsibility. Obviously the ideal would be to establish some senior management sponsorship of your activity. It would allow you to go further and to have a much wider impact in the organization. Yet, even if you start with your own area, you can make a substantial contribution and persuade others by your own example. So in approaching this stocktake make a decision about how broad your approach is going to be and then use it to establish an achievable action plan.

STOCKTAKE 10: ADDRESSING THE ETHICAL DILEMMAS

There is no easy answer or simple process by which you will end up with a set of ethical principles. There are, however, a number of issues where by reviewing current practice and setting a standard you can develop a set of action-oriented principles that will form the basis of a broader set of values that can be exported across the organization.

■ Start with the obvious: list your major suppliers and contractors. Against each one note any actions they have taken in the last twelve months in order to encourage you or colleagues to continue to utilize their products or services.

	Contractor	*Actions*
1		
2		
3		
4		
5		
etc.		

■ Now, taking those actions, ask yourself the following: Do I feel that those actions were 'over the top' or that they placed me in a position where I was then expected to respond to this activity rather than to the quality of the product/service? Split the actions into Yes and No columns.

	Yes	*No*
1		
2		
3		
4		
5		
etc.		

■ Taking the two lists, draw out up to five reasons to why actions appeared in the Yes as opposed to the No column.

1

2

3

4

5

■ Looking at the key differences, now establish a standard for each area which you feel would ensure that promotional activity such as hospitality, Christmas gifts, etc., would meet your 'No' criteria:

1

2

3

4

5

■ Taking your five standards as a base point, now share these thoughts with your manager, a colleague and a friend in another organization who you believe would be facing a similar set of issues. Ask them to agree, disagree, amend and add to your list. Note their reactions here:

1   Manager

2   Colleague

3   Friend

■ Given the above what would be your list of standards?

1

2

3

4

5

etc.

■ Now review how you operate in respect of your own customers, employees and other functions and in respect of the public, community organizations, etc., using these basic standards. What do you currently do which does not meet these standards or does not meet standards already set in respect of, say, payment periods for suppliers, respect for community views, etc.? List the ten most obvious areas and what would have to change in order to get a closer alignment with these standards.

Activity	*Required changes*
1	
2	
3	
4	
5	
6	
7	
8	
9	
10	

■ Take all those you can change for yourself and establish an action timetable for making those changes. Remember, part of the timetable should include clear and concise communication of the standard you are expecting people to achieve and how you will monitor it. Make it clear what the consequences are for non-compliance.

Action	*Timing*	*Communicate to:*
1		
2		

3

4

5

etc.

■ Now take three areas where someone else has the authority and establish a similar action plan, identifying who needs to be persuaded and what you think are the most telling arguments for the business in making the changes you are proposing. Start with the easy wins – and keep reviewing progress.

	Action required	*Agreement required from*	*Timing*
1			
2			
3			
4			
5			
etc.			

AND AFTER ALL THAT?

The importance of environmental and ethical issues for businesses of all sizes and for public-sector organizations is going to become a major management activity by the year 2000. We will need to consider how best we introduce these concepts into development activities, appraisals and recruitment policies to ensure that our organizations develop a competitive edge in this respect.

What it also means is increasing importance being placed on communities either where the organization is based or from where it derives substantial income or benefit. The commitment to and management of community affairs will become another factor by which we as managers will be judged by the general public. This in itself only serves to reinforce the growth of the concept of stakeholders in a business other than just shareholders. Stakeholders, as the word implies, are those who have a stake in the organization's continued success. For some of these groups, however, success is not just going to be measured in simple profit terms. Rather environmental impact, investment policies, job security, community sensitivity will all become terms as familiar to management goals as income, profit and cash. If you are doubtful, then take a look at the latest annual reports from the top fifty UK and US companies.

Having said all this, it is still going to be a long haul: in the most recent research reported[3] it seems that the UK's senior management, although recognizing the issues, still feel little inclination to act. The research team are quoted as saying: 'Clearly managers feel the social and political responsibilities of the Nineties are outside their field of influence.' If business does not wake up to the need to act in these areas then I fear society will act on its behalf.

6 Learning to break the rules: the potential impact of information systems

For many businesses information systems are a misnomer. They are at best weapons in the control armoury of the finance community, and at worst provide streams of data none of which is in any way informative. Yet the application of technology already available could give an organization real competitive advantage. At an individual level proper exploitation of the terminal which sits on the desk could equally powerfully improve performance.

Information, the need for more and more of it and the increasing speed at which it is required, must be one of the biggest single contributors to management stress. Unless we are careful we drown in it. Drown not only because of the volume which is on offer but also because of the manner in which it is presented and because we really do not understand what precisely it is we should be looking for.

The reason for this lies in the history of the information systems function, which in nearly all organizations started life, if it does not still reside, in the finance function. As was pointed out earlier in the book, finance has at its worst been mostly about control and little about risk and opportunity, so the information systems activity was predominantly directed at such control and monitoring activity as finance felt appropriate. I appreciate here I am ignoring the development of process control systems but I do so to concentrate on what until recently have passed for management information systems.

Systems directed at control and monitoring are basically translations of previous manual processes or they are externally bought-in systems where management processes have been altered to fit the system purchased. The latter normally means more work for

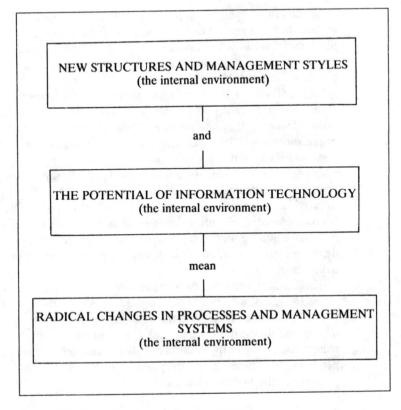

Figure 6.1 New technology and management

managers, increased bureaucracy and a reduction in overall efficiency, although the reports look great and contain anything you
may ever want to know – although nothing you really need to
know!

History therefore tells us that until recently we have been
automating business as usual. However, to build and sustain real
competitive advantage a business must identify its core competences and work to develop these. In doing so we must also
consider the whole range of activity in those areas where, by
changing current business processes to take account of developments in the external environment in which we operate, we could
establish a competitive advantage in the marketplace.

Successful organizations in the twenty-first century will need to be lean but still ensure that key business functions are close to the markets in which they operate; able to respond rapidly to new opportunities and changes in the market; and adopt business processes that enable rapid change and development rather than hinder it. The potential for information systems is to move towards a role where they support these integrating goals across organizations, ensuring that one of the core competences of all successful organizations will be in the management of information and the systems by which it is provided.

Innovative and timely application of relevant information throughout organizations will be a fundamental building block in improving competitiveness. This will mean that eventually it will become essential for information systems to move out of the orbit of finance and be seen as a powerful and independent unit that can drive an organization considerably faster than it does at present in many cases.

Establishing information systems functions which are of equal status to others, with board representation, is one structural answer to this challenge. However, the real task is to start to break the management continuum that sees a system as a way of rationalizing what is currently undertaken. If we can achieve this we can genuinely re-engineer organizations so that they can begin to perform to the highest standards.

PROCESSES, NOT PROCEDURES

The task of management succeeds or fails depending on the efficacy of the processes that support the activity being managed. If there are no clear processes for communicating changes in priorities, for reviewing sales figures and acting upon the information, for involving the right people at the right stage to obtain a commitment to a course of action, then managers become only as effective as their own personal skills in these areas will allow. For an organization to make a significant difference it has to establish sequences of related tasks and functions which together produce outcomes that contribute to success.

Most businesses have automated their important, usually financial, processes. What they have done, however, is in most cases to automate principles that were established with the scientific schools of management in the early 1900s. We have applied information technology – sometimes with the systems equivalent of brute force – to what currently exists and have as a consequence masked many of the real shortcomings in the way we operate. No doubt we have achieved some improvements in operating speed, and sometimes cost, and hence believe that our systems are truly effective. The truth, however, is much more likely to be that the underlying process is neolithic and our automation has done nothing to add real value or competitive edge.

In this book we have reviewed areas where accepted principles and approaches will no longer serve to sustain successful organizations. Indeed many of the processes that will be developed as a result of taking account of the issues discussed here will require organizations to break their continuous thinking of the last thirty years. They need to take a leap that will enable them to create possibilities, to establish a vision of an integrated organization which can respond and develop in response to the environment in which it finds itself.

This requires change. Our business systems on the whole have not been designed to change, however, and the assumptions and rules that applied for the last thirty years or so have been built right through the system. Indeed many organizations' systems were designed *not* to change. The system in itself prevents us from seeing opportunities for change. How often do we hear the cry 'You can't do that, it will mean changing the system'?

What we have done in fact is to set in concrete a raft of procedures rather than expedite an essential business process. Why? Because we have not looked beyond what is already possible. We have looked only at our own function or area of responsibility. We do not look broadly at the organization, its purpose, its declared strategy and how our operation or area impacts on, and adds value to, that strategy. We look only at improving what we do now, not at what we could do if we had the capacity in systems.

RE-ENGINEERING THE ORGANIZATION

The essence of a 'new age' information system is that it must be organically designed for change. It has to have a capacity to adapt. Change therefore needs to be built into the system, not treated as an irritating afterthought. Systems that support management processes must have a capacity for continuous review in order to improve. Imagine the power of an organization that had that ability.

Where the costs of labour, resources, materials, etc., have been at the centre of the management agenda, in the twenty-first century management concentration will be on the most efficient utilization of all assets. Effectiveness will come from empowering managers, decentralizing and delegating power and generating understanding of, and commitment to, the core competences and strategic intent of the business. It follows that the organizational structures and work practices of such an organization will have to be different from those that worked in the old control environments. Re-engineering provides the opportunity to develop processes that enable the new organization to manage successfully in the new environment. Keeping today's systems and attempting to manage tomorrow's business will eventually place you in yesterday's competition.

To re-engineer an organization what is required is a bottom-up review of business processes and an understanding of the links that will enable us to reconsider what we are currently doing in the light of what we are trying to achieve. The review should consider the possible impact of information systems on developing new ways of operating which would significantly enhance the effectiveness of the operation. At times this will require thinking outside the boundaries set by the business and being given permission to 'break the rules'.

Examples of potential technologies that have yet to be applied to anything like their full effect are:

■ Electronic mail, where not only can paperwork and the processing behind it be substantially reduced but significant and influential links with suppliers and customers can be forged by connecting them to your system. At GrandMet Estates we linked major solicitors' offices to our own legal department and found ourselves with a very powerful and efficient conveyancing process that until then had been nothing but a source of considerable irritation to potential lessees, the solicitors and ourselves.

■ Document imaging, which allows a single document to be in more than one place at the same time. It offers immense potential for the restructuring of work processes, particularly giving opportunities to concertina document processing to reduce delays. In addition pictorial information can be held and accessed along with type-script, providing a very powerful management tool enabling decisions to be taken more quickly and at a level where there is complete local knowledge.

■ Interactive video and interactive laser-discs, which currently are employed in training and in activities such as company communi-cations. We have yet to think through the implications of its potential to replace people as we come increasingly under the demographic pressures discussed earlier.

Exploiting these developments to re-engineer our business to enable us to adapt and change will require continuous learning and development. A system is only as good as those who manage it.

The potential for information systems to add significantly more value to organizations than many already do is substantial. The challenge we face as managers is taking the first steps towards unlocking that potential in our own areas of responsibility. It is clear that it is up to us to understand the basics of the technologies available – and of those soon to be available – and to initiate process reviews. Faced with this vast canvas we can become cautious and decide to wait or to set up review groups or to refer the matter ever upwards (or sideways or downwards, just so long as you do not ask me to make a decision ...). Competitive advantage, however, rests with those who take the initiative and it is more than possible to take some simple first steps which will begin a move towards re-engineering.

ACTION STEPS

Separating the data from the information

Data is not information. It only becomes information if it tells you something against which you can take decisions. Most of us receive plenty of data. We get budget reports, sales reports, salary data, reports on competitors, etc. What we then do with the data is try to make sense of it. It is never presented in quite the way we want, nor does it cover the entirety of what we need; and, of course, we will need something slightly different again and will want another perspective on the same figures. We need therefore to be absolutely clear as to what information we require to achieve the outcomes that are expected of us.

Establishing the information flows

Information from random or inappropriate sources is not useful. In fact it can be positively dangerous. Not getting what you need to know from where you need to know it is a common problem. Mapping the information flows that should support your particular activity is essential to understanding how the business processes that are employed in your organization could be radically enhanced through the use of information systems.

If flows in to you are essential, so are flows out from your area to others. Managers must be prepared to ensure they are aware of all those to whom they should provide information and the content and levels of detail required. This takes a real shift in management attitudes in some quarters, given that many units – particularly those in local markets away from a head office or those with specialist responsibility – prefer to keep as much information within their control as possible. Transparency, however, is a requirement if effective and timely decisions are to be made which will ensure a fast response to the customer. Withholding information can only put achievement of the organization's objectives at even greater risk.

Identifying information blockages

It is likely that there will be processes operating in any organization that block necessary information from appearing in a timely fashion or from appearing at all. Decision-making processes are often the major culprits in this respect, along with those processes designed to link the customer and/or consumer with those responsible for quality and service. Information, particularly when it is referring to a complaint or a problem, has a habit of getting bogged down in a backwater, or just plain 'lost in the system'. Blockages can be caused by too many unnecessary people in the 'loop'; authority levels being too high, requiring sign-offs from senior people in other offices, and distance and time zone changes can mean documentation taking twice as long to process and deliver back to the office requiring it. Additionally, organizations can be structured to service a forgotten principle established years previously by a management long since gone.

Looking for internal linkages

Internal linkages are likely to occur for two reasons: either you will have a common database need, although the application of that database to provide relevant information may well be very different; or you will contribute to a common task, although from differing databases. We will need to establish where, although there should be a link, there is none. Failing to recognize and manage these links leads to a whole range of problems: different data being applied to the same issue, causing disputes and confusion; the same task being carried out in different areas because data is not being made available, and time and distance creating tensions amongst those who share a common task such as supplying customers. All of these areas could be addressed through an information systems solution, which may require a very different management approach but will mean a quantum leap in effectiveness.

Looking for external opportunities

There are substantial advantages to be gained from cementing key customers and suppliers and potentially influential customer groups to your data network. Certainly those aspects which deal with communication, ordering, stock control, billing and credit and customer service could add significant competitive advantage. They will bind these key organizations into your own, making it much more difficult for them to 'go elsewhere' and building a climate of partnership where problems are resolved and there is a perceptible advantage in staying together.

Robert Haas, CEO of Levi Strauss & Co., talked about developing a systems linkage with suppliers and customers in an interview published in the USA. The payback he quotes is that customers operated with 20–30 per cent less stock and achieved 20–30 per cent better sales. He talks of a 'seamless partnership, with interrelationships and mutual commitments right through the chain that would have been unimaginable ten years previously'. The implications for jobs and processes are fundamental: 'Our employees have many more responsibilities ... the work is much more creative, more entrepreneurial. It's as if these people are in business for themselves. They're doing what human beings do best – think, plan, interact, see trends, humanize the business to make it more successful.'[1]

These straightforward steps are management tasks which allow organizations to exploit the technological potential that integrated information systems can offer. In a world where the need for and speed of information are increasing, organizations that fail to see this potential and make the necessary investment will begin to fall behind their more forward-thinking competition.

STOCKTAKE 11: THINKING OUTSIDE THE BOX

If data and process are the fundamentals of successful management information systems then it is important that you consider your own area of responsibility in the four stages outlined above before starting to think of the possible answers. The challenge is to think outside the box and to look for connections and possibilities that up to now you have never seen or considered. If it helps, clear your own head by writing down all the possible answers you currently have in your head – just brainstorm them and note them in any order below

1

2

3

4

5

etc.

It may be that none of these address the real problems or they merely automate what has gone before; however, you should return to them at the end of this stocktake after you have completed your initial review. First you need to map out exactly what information you believe you require to meet your own and your department's required outputs:

■ Note your main activities. Against each activity list the information you need to perform successfully.

	Activity	*Required information*
1		
2		
3		
4		
5		
etc.		

■ Taking the required information: where should you get it from?

	Required information	*Ideal source*
1		
2		
3		
4		
5		
etc.		

■ To whom should you be providing information, what do they need and why are you providing it?

	Information	*To whom*	*Why*
1			
2			
3			
4			
5			
etc.			

■ What information do you currently get/send, from/to whom and when?

Information	*From/To whom*	*When*
1		
2		
3		
4		
5		

etc.

■ Where are the gaps between what you should receive/send and what you currently get/send? Note gaps in terms of content, format and regularity/availability.

Information required	*Available*	*Gaps*
1		
2		
3		
4		
5		

etc.

■ Where in your own experience do information blockages occur currently that frustrate you and/or your department in achieving your goals?

1

2

3

4

5

etc.

■ With whom should you share a common database?

1

2

3

4

5

etc.

■ With whom do you share common tasks or contribute to a larger task?

1

2

3

4

5

etc.

■ Looking at the answers to the last two questions, what are the links between you and those listed in respect of both process and data?

Department/Team/   *Data/Process links*
Function

1

2

3

4

5

etc.

■ For each link what would make a significant difference
   if you could change either data flows or management
   processes?

   Link   *Change required*

1

2

3

4

5

etc.

■ What external parties with whom you have regular and
   significant contact would benefit if they were linked to
   your management information systems? How would you
   benefit?

   Party   *Benefit to them*   *Benefit to you*

1

2

3

4

5

etc.

■ You have now identified the basis of an action plan.
   There will obviously be some major knock-ons,
   particularly with the areas of internal and external links,
   but there will also be action plans that can be firmed up

with your IS function and with your own management that will in themselves make a significant impact on how you operate. List here all those areas you have identified that you feel you could take on within your own sphere of influence. Identify at least one action you will take for each area.

Area	Action identified
1	
2	
3	
4	
5	
etc.	

■ Now list the others and against each one decide how best to process your ideas. It is at this stage you should involve the IS team and the specialists as well as your wider network. It may well be that your own IS people have been trying to find a champion for this activity ... here's your chance.

Area	Action identified
1	
2	
3	
4	
5	
etc.	

What you have just completed is a very simple beginning to a systems plan that aims to integrate information systems into the overall strategy of the business so that the support provided by information is directed at the outcomes the organization wants to achieve. It is impossible here to offer even simple solutions or to take your thinking further without you plugging into your specialist resources and involving the wider management group. However, it could be the most significant thing you contribute to your organization if you can start the process whereby it looks at how it could re-engineer to support its competitive position.

ENHANCING YOUR OWN EFFECTIVENESS

Many of us now have computer terminals or PCs sitting on our desks or on the desks of staff who work for us. Despite the arguments above, a real opportunity lies in auditing what you currently do via paper systems to see whether there is a capacity for improving your own or your department's effectiveness. For example:

- Budget control and monitoring via spreadsheets
- Mailing lists for regular addressees – internal or external via a mail/merge process
- Installing word-processing 'macros' that automatically set up memos, letters, etc., in the right place for the paper
- Downloading data from mainframes automatically on to spreadsheets for easier and speedier manipulation
- Producing your own graphics and overhead slides

Most of us have yet to understand anything like the full potential of the machine on the desk. The software we have installed is probably used for nothing like its full potential and we have never really spent time reading the manual to find out what it can do. This could well be the opportunity to establish links with your IT/IS department. Ask them to audit what is on your machines, what you use them for currently and could they suggest what you could do to improve their effectiveness in this regard. Then ask them to explain what possibilities exist: perhaps other departments have already developed applications which could help you.

Establishing this as a base may take some time – but it will be essential if you are to be able to take the bigger steps involved in a significant shift in the application of your information systems.

7 Standards, measurement and reward: moving from prescription to empowerment

It is essential for a modern business to do more than just hope that it recruits and trains the best possible people. Increasingly it is becoming clear that the real winners are those who have a precise idea of what is vital to their success and have established key standards throughout their operations to reinforce their ability to compete effectively.

RJR Nabisco's CEO, Lou Gerstner, is quoted as stating that 'you can outmanage your competition by having brilliant strategies, but those brilliant strategies have to be executed brilliantly'.[1] In other words sustainable competitive advantage can only be achieved if you ensure the skills at the very core of your business are understood and given a very clear focus. These core skills are usually referred to as core competences. They will be both technical (e.g. the skills needed to be a proficient, engineer, marketer, etc.) and managerial.

Why managerial? Little successful has been achieved in any organization unless it has the management capability to deliver effective performance. We can understand that we need to have 'leading edge' technology, but unless we can plan its introduction, think through the organizational consequences and gain the commitment of those who have to work with it, then it will never deliver the enhanced performance we were hoping for. That requires brilliant management execution. There is a clear link therefore between competitiveness and effective management.

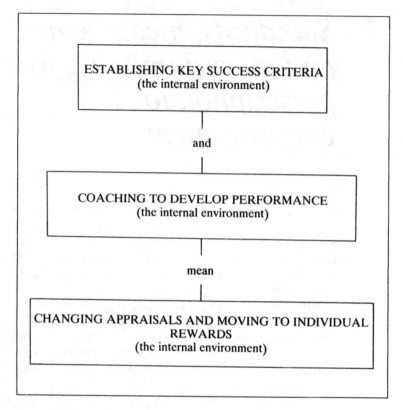

Figure 7.1 Stages in moving from prescription to empowerment

DEFINING STANDARDS FOR SUCCESS

To define and build these skills throughout a business requires managers to think about the organization as a whole rather than the people within it and to think of their organization's ability to compete. What that means, for example, is asking the question 'Do we have the ability to set clear and meaningful performance objectives?' rather than 'Do we have good appraisers?'

The key to understanding competence is to understand what the company will need to do *better* than the competition in order to reach peak performance. In the context of management competence this means establishing organization-wide best practice in those areas most closely associated with the delivery of individual performance. Technically/professionally, it will mean understanding precisely what the organization requires and then developing a level of proficiency that is consistently above that achieved by the competition.

Essentially this will require us to develop what we currently accept as performance criteria and to consider changes and additions to them in recognition of the new skills that organizations will require to meet the challenges of the 1990s. Those challenges highlight the core management competence areas that we need to consider as we review our own organizations to understand what is core and therefore should be given a particular focus.

- The demographic and ecological issues will call for flexible, imaginative and creative responses from all managers.
- The establishment of a learning approach will require coaching and development skills.
- The changes in organizational structures and management styles require influencing, communication, team working and listening skills.
- Information systems and the re-engineering of our businesses will require an awareness of the application and, importantly, the organizational impact of the IT decisions with which we will all be faced.
- Coming to terms with ethics in the organization and the establishment of ethical standards will require greater individual responsibility for decisions.
- The rise of the individual and the move from control cultures to those based on commitment will require delegation of authority, trust and a significant degree of openness.
- Change management in itself is a skill covering planning, organization, visioning, listening and sensitive implementation skills.
- It is also clear that results-oriented performance management will remain a fundamental for all successful businesses.

If, as I contend, you believe that developing organizations in the directions contained above is an essential part of establishing sustainable competitive advantage, then the core management competences that we need to establish will be based on the skills outlined above.

However, these are still very general statements. Most of us can agree with 'highest standards of team working', for example. But what exactly does it mean in the context of the organization we work for? To establish this we must begin to set some standards that explain to people what we mean and give guidance that enables them to appreciate their strengths and development needs. What we have to do is to look at our own organization or a sub-set of the organization and establish some definitions of success.

STOCKTAKE 12: DEFINING CORE COMPETENCES AND SUCCESS MEASURES

■ Write down what your organization is attempting to achieve

1

2

3

4

5

etc.

■ What role does your area of responsibility contribute to this overall objective?

1

2

3

4

5

etc.

■   What are the core activities that are required of your
    area in order to make its proper contribution to the
    organizations objectives?

1

2

3

4

5

etc.

■   Rank your activities in descending order of importance

1

2

3

4

5

etc.

■   Now take the top five. Taking each activity, identify any
    technical/professional/business skill that is essential for
    individuals to perform effectively. Then consider what
    managerial or personal skills are required for individuals
    to perform effectively. List them on the table below

Activity	*Technical/ Professional*	*Management/ Personal*
1		
2		
3		
4		
5		
etc.		

■ List any skills that appeared more than once

    Technical, etc.   *Management/Personal*

1

2

3

4

5

■ Now take each skill and determine what you consider to be your success standards for that skill. What do you expect? How will you know what success will look/feel like?

    Technical skill 1   *Management skill 1*

    Required standards   Required standards

1

2

3

4

5

    What will success   What will success
    look like?   look like?

1

2

3

4

5

Technical skill 2   *Management skill 2*

Required standards   Required standards

1

2

3

4

5

What will success   What will success
look like?   look like?

1

2

3

4

5

Technical skill 3   *Management skill 3*

Required standards   Required standards

1

2

3

4

5

What will success   What will success
look like?   look like?

1

2

3

4

5

Technical skill 4   *Management skill 4*

Required standards   Required standards

1

2

3

4

5

What will success   What will success
look like?   look like?

1

2

3

4

5

Technical skill 5   *Management skill 5*

Required standards   Required standards

1

2

3

4

5

What will success   What will success
look like?   look like?

1

2

3

4

5

What you have established in Stocktake 12 is a list of core competences with a definition of the standards you believe are important and a description of what you would expect to see if these skills were being employed successfully.

What you should do now is think about your area of responsibility and check whether or not you have already established these core competences in yourself and your team. Are your team aware of what you are judging success by in these key areas? Is your own manager aware of what you think is vital and what standards you are expecting?

It is likely that for many of us the answer in some areas will be 'no'. What if it is? Success will have come if we have thought through these issues for ourselves and have pinpointed our own development areas. The next step is to look around for a suitable coach to help overcome key barriers. Revisit Stocktake 5 and ensure you reflect any new insights from this process in your own analysis of your strengths and development needs.

In addition to doing this personally you should review objectives agreed with team members and with your manager to ensure they really reflect what it is you need to do 'brilliantly'. Offer yourself as a coach to the team in areas where they need to develop.

APPRAISING AND DEVELOPING CORE COMPETENCES

Organizational performance can be enhanced significantly if managers focus, and get others to focus, on a small number of core skills which have to be carried out to the highest standards. For most organizations the primary mechanism for achieving this focus is a performance appraisal. Most appraisal systems are perfectly adequate. Where they fail time and time again is in the skills, or rather lack of them, of those entrusted to carry out the appraisal. This lack of skill in the appraiser is compounded with an equal lack of skill in the appraisee.

It is not my intention here to launch, therefore, into a guide to researching, designing and launching appraisal systems; rather to concentrate on some key areas which if addressed would significantly increase the likelihood of an appraisal process having a major (and positive) impact on performance, regardless of the system being used.

Essentially, appraisal is simple. We take pleasure, however, in turning it into an administrative and operational nightmare. Forms of every hue and length, guidelines which confuse more than they clarify, have all been the stuff from which empires have grown. Most managers find annual performance appraisals the most difficult and unwelcome task they have to perform. A business could ease this burden if it considered the following points.

ACTION STEPS

Remove the confusion as to purpose

Why do we have appraisal systems? Fundamentally, if you look back at the development of management processes, because of a continued desire to have an obvious link between pay and performance. They are the tools of a control-based culture that requires information to justify pay awards under compensation schemes that award more to high performers.

We also, however, have them to focus on development needs. How, not just what, did we perform and what areas of our personal or technical skills could we improve? They are also tools, therefore, of a development culture designed to focus individuals on their own contributions and how they could be enhanced.

They are also, for many of us, the mechanism by which career aspirations are raised – if only to be dashed by inept career planning or poor management of expectations. We use them to record career potential and to assess that potential – in a lot of systems this part of the process is either half in the shadows or 'closed', leaving us entirely in the dark. So they are also tools of the development and succession planners whose needs are highly specific and whose results are often inaccessible.

There is therefore a substantial chance that in the minds of the managers who have to utilize appraisals there is considerable confusion as to the purpose of the exercise they are undertaking. It is time that organizations reviewed their appraisal systems and clearly defined their purpose.

In a high-performing organization committed to personal growth and development, appraisal should serve only two purposes: recognition of an individual's performance and feedback on areas of strength and on areas requiring greater development. The review of strengths and development needs to be focused on those core competences the organization values as significant contributors to sustaining competitive advantage. These purposes should be clearly separated and ideally the discussions should be held at separate times. In this way we would make a clear distinction between reviewing performance in order to make a judgement on pay and reviewing development and personal growth in order to improve the long-term contribution of the individual concerned.

Stamp out ineffective and unjustified measurement

Most managers set poor quality objectives. They do not define the task they wish to see addressed. They use words that defy assessment – 'review', 'manage', etc., – rather than words that clearly state what is required. Most managers refer only to time. Fewer make any broad reference to quantity. Very few refer to cost, quality and to the management of resources. The result of this inability to define a measurable objective is a highly subjective review of performance. If you have not agreed a clear set of targets that can be measured with the individual you are appraising, then the potential for disputes is enormous.

This, however, should not limit performance appraisal to the purely quantitative. Qualitative aspects are not only very important but they can also be measured effectively. If you want someone to improve their relationships with customers, for example, then you should define what you would see, hear or feel[2] if they were to be successful. Having defined the requirements, you can measure them: better customer relations could mean fewer customer complaints – easily assessed.

Reduce the annual bureaucratic paper-chase

In a review of public-sector organizations in the United Kingdom conducted in the mid-1980s the authors concluded that appraisal systems had degenerated into a sterile paper-chase which contributed little to the quality of organizational performance. 'Appraisal in practice,' they argued, 'tends to become a grand annual convulsion, more of a bureaucratic colossus than a means of ensuring continued development of people.'[3]

No doubt for most of us this would form a fitting epitaph on the vast majority of the appraisal systems under which we have been assessed. The more management have found the process difficult and unrewarding, the more the HR function have added guidelines, rules, controls and additional paper to ensure managers carry it out.

Replace annual appraisal skills with regular feedback and coaching skills

What very few organizations have recognized is that there are alternatives, far more effective for improving organizational performance, than this annual bureaucrats' paradise. Feedback on performance is necessary, not just to place decisions on salary or bonus awards in context. It also indicates where behaviours contribute to success or failure and how to address those areas where behaviours could be changed to improve overall performance.

It is accepted that for feedback on behaviour to be really effective – particularly if it is aimed at changing behaviour – it has to be as near as possible to the time at which the observation was made. In other words, saving it up for the annual review and releasing it as an enormous critical dump is counterproductive. It is this that I believe is at the heart of the skills issue. If we can skill managers to a level where they are happy to give and receive continuous feedback and can then coach their subordinates on a regular basis, we will make far greater strides towards effective appraisal.[4]

In this way all an annual appraisal becomes is the summary of all the regular feedback and coaching discussions held during the year. No surprises, no recriminations and plenty of focus on developing individuals to improve their performance.

David Maitland, a UK management development consultant, has presented the key issues in a challenging way as follows.

PERFORMANCE REVIEW

Isn't	*Is*
A bureaucratic ritual designed by the personnel department to meet its own agenda at the expense of the organization's producers.	The single most effective tool available to any line manager for getting more of what he wants from those who work for him.

A unilateral determination of ability and conformity to unspecified, subjective and arbitrary standards of good performance.

A bilateral analysis of rational people of the recent contributions of one of them to the aims of the other and agreement as to how that contribution can be increased.

An ordeal with the Spanish Inquisition.

Relaxing with your doubles partner after the match to savour your more successful tactics and refine the less successful.

Imposition of objectives so that, when they have been missed, they can be recited to justify summary and unfair treatment.

An opportunity to reconcile expectations and the developing ambitions of employer and employee to the greatest advantage of both.

The AGM of a mutual admiration society, or the reopening and application of salt to the wounds of a personality clash.

A mature, continuing discussion of personal style to exploit complementary strengths and minimise irritation.

Irreconcilable demands for the resources to permit additional performance, and for the performance to justify additional resources.

A professional analysis of the new resources which might be made available and how they could be justified.

Concerned with why the Creator gave people the personalities they have.

Concerned with what people actually do and how their behaviour might be more effective.

The failure year after year to mention the real barrier to praise and promotion, in the hope that it will vanish miraculously.

The reassurance of knowing the real agenda is on the table and both parties are committed to tackling it in co-operation.

An exercise in alienation, leaving reviewees feeling

An exercise in motivation, leaving reviewees feeling

bewildered, bruised, baffled and betrayed.	appreciated, clear, committed and enthusiastic.
The partnership meeting at which the rewards of past performance are allocated by process of recrimination and direct comparison.	The robust discussion, gentle with people and tough with problems, without which effective teamwork is impossible.
Concluded with unaccountable expressions of goodwill and intentions fit only to pave the road to hell.	Recorded in the form of agreed proposals for action, the dates by which action will have been taken, and a basis for monitoring it.

STOCKTAKE 13: EFFECTIVE PERFORMANCE REVIEW

If a significant component of competitive advantage is identifying the core competences and then setting objectives that define key success measurements, effective reviews of performance are essential. How else will you and others know how close you are getting to the required standard?

Performance appraisals need not be a nightmare – whatever system you are required to act under – and although your system may require development to meet the key requirements I have outlined for success you can still make a powerful difference to your organization's ability to perform by carrying out effective performance reviews.

This stocktake takes you through a planning process for a performance review that can be part of your appraisal process or part of a regular review conducted with a direct subordinate or someone with whom you have a working relationship where influencing is the only way that performance can be affected.

■ Take your most challenging appraisee (or only one!) or your most difficult working relationship where performance needs to be improved

■ Establish five positive outcomes which you wish to achieve from this discussion

1

2

3

4

5

■ What are their strengths? Give examples from the last six months

1

2

3

4

5

etc.

■ What are their development needs? Give examples from the last six months

1

2

3

4

5

etc.

Having regard to the above . . .

■ What do they do currently that hinders their performance?

1

2

3

4

5

etc.

■ What should they do that would enhance their performance?

1

2

3

4

5

etc.

■ What do they currently do that they should continue doing, as it enhances their performance?

1

2

3

4

5

etc.

■ Think of ten questions that you could ask them that would help them understand your appraisal of their performance in the light of the above

1

2

3

4

5

6

7

8

9

10

■ Using questions that get them to appraise themselves, how would you structure such a feedback session to ensure that it focuses on the key issues you have highlighted? Plan your approach using the framework below.

1   *Set the context* Explain here why you are holding the review and set some ground rules about recording outcomes, etc.

2   *Gaining their views* Start by asking for their view of their performance. This is where your ten questions will play a major role. Wait for cues to introduce specific questions, e.g. 'I think that I could do more planning' – reply 'What did you think of your planning in the last sales period?'

3   *Giving your reaction and views* Having heard them out – it shows respect for them, you are valuing their opinion – then give your reactions. Keep these factual and focused, using the evidence you have recorded above.

4   *Exploring how they feel/see things* Before assuming your perceptions were totally right it is important to give the reviewee time to react, explain and tell you how they feel about your feedback – positive and negative.

5   *Identifying performance barriers* It is important to try to explore why if the reviewee is not meeting your standards they are having difficulty.

6   *Helping them find solutions* Having established possible barriers, get them to generate possible solutions first before imposing your own orthodoxy: it will gain far greater commitment.

7   *Agreeing action plans* Having got solutions, you can now agree a set of objectives – which may include you coaching more regularly – which will ensure an improvement in performance.

THE CONSEQUENCES FOR REWARD AND MOTIVATION

The introduction of core competences, and the effective management of performance against them have significant consequences for the ways in which we traditionally reward and motivate employees.

Goodbye, job evaluation . . .

I believe they signal the death knell for job evaluation in its current form. Three cheers, say I. Nothing can be more counterproductive than asking someone to write a job description. In itself it is a thankless task. More important in today's businesses, it is a nigh-on impossible one. Jobs change rapidly in content, emphasis and even skill requirements. Organizations change regularly, impacting on reporting relationships and scope of responsibility.

Even more significant with the rise of individually focused reward is that it has become increasingly obvious that the relative worth, and contribution, of a job can be affected dramatically by the person who holds it. You can have two managers on a supposedly equal footing, one of whom is contributing more and taking more responsibility because they are far more competent. There is no way you should reward these two equally. Under most job evaluation systems you have no choice but to keep them within relative parity.

What should change? Well, fundamentally we should evaluate the individual, not the job, as the job is the individual. Against what? Against the core competences which we decide are key to our business success. How? By using effective performance review and by establishing competence standards which will differ significantly depending on broad levels within the organization.

. . . and goodbye, collective reward

If individual competence is to be rewarded, then the key to motivation is to reward individually. This will require a compensation revolution that is only just beginning to be envisaged in a handful of organizations.

Known as 'cafeteria compensation', flexible reward schemes can take several forms. The essence, however, of all the schemes so far implemented is to provide an individually tailored reward, within a framework. Up till now most human resources departments have fiercely resisted any move towards flexibility, preferring to reward the job rather than the individual performance. However, as market pressures build through demographic changes successful high performers will move to where they perceive they will get the greatest recognition. It is not necessarily the highest payer who will win: it will be the organization that best reflects the needs of the individual concerned. As we move to develop individual potential we must have a parallel development to ensure there is individual recognition of that development.

One final thought: with flat structures, greater lateral movement and the growth of two or three careers during a working lifetime, job evaluation and ridged pay policies will start to work against the organizations we are trying to establish.

Core competences, once established, have to form the basis of all the key people systems and activities in an organization if they are to succeed in making their establishment and successful application the basis for sustained competitive advantage.

Competence, however requires companies to invest in assets like systems and training, and these investments will be less easy to justify to City analysts and wary shareholders, as they are less tangible than capital investments and they depress short-term profits. However, it is only by taking such action that we will be able to build the necessary organizational capability to respond with the speed and creativity demanded by the competitive environment of the future.

Competence, then, is all-embracing: it should form the basis of recruitment decisions – we should not be recruiting those who either do not display or do not have the potential to display skills in our core areas. Additionally it has to form the basis of development activities. Not just those associated with formal appraisal but also those associated with the setting of career paths. This in itself will require a move to individual evaluation and reward. What competences also point to is the establishment of functional, and cross-functional, career paths which map out the experience that will develop and enhance the core functional and management competences needed to succeed.

By setting core competences in the manner described the organization has laid the basis for a very significant standard in itself: it has laid down a common language in which these common standards can be discussed and applied to individual assessment.

8 Developing a climate of success: the challenge of organizational culture

Businesses are going to have to face a continuous process of change as they progress through to the twenty-first century. The change that many will need to achieve if they are to take on the issues raised in this book alone is not just in management processes and structures, patterns of employment, etc. It is an overall shift in the approach to management. Successfully facing up to the challenges covered in this book will result in a significant shift in culture. By developing self-reliant managers who are able and willing to address these issues at all levels of an organization we will be establishing powerful change agents who can make the difference between success and failure. Their actions will of themselves develop a climate of success.

It is important for us to recognize the power and complexity of organizational culture and to judge for ourselves how much of a challenge we will be taking on as we look to make changes in our own areas and to influence change across the organization as a whole.[1]

THE 'C' WORD

Corporate culture, like any other culture, revolves around a set of inherent values that in some way are perpetuated by each generation – in the case of an organization each generation of management. The key to understanding why a group is a group is to appreciate that its members are brought together through *shared* values.

Think about this for yourself: bring to mind one of your good

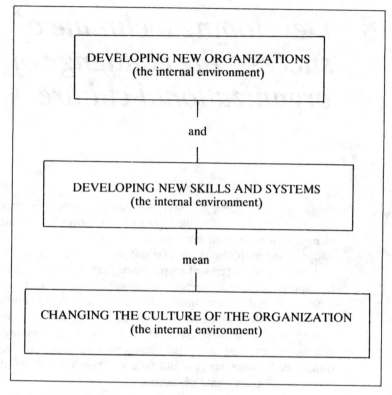

Figure 8.1 The challenge of organizational culture

friends, either inside or outside work, think about the job they do, the paper they read, the car they drive, where they live and the clubs they have joined. In the first instance they may be quite similar to yourself, for, although diverse in many ways, nationalities share certain key values.

But although it gives us things in common we cannot choose our nationality: we accept the basic values and attitudes as we are brought up, primarily subconsciously. As we develop, however, we do start to make choices based on the value system which we establish for ourselves. By the time we leave school we already have a personal value system, either inherited from our parents or developed in reaction to them. A good example of this is the newspapers we choose to read: we read the newspaper we agree with. We don't buy it if we know we are going to disagree. In other words, they reflect the values that we already hold. But newspapers are, however, an individual choice.

We also choose to join with others whose values are the same as ours and who do things in the way that we would. We join a club, either a social one like a working men's club or one that, although essentially focused on an activity, also represents a value to others with whom we mix, such as a golf club. The clubs we decide to join attract people who have at least one value in common. That is why we join them: we feel we could fit in there. We choose to live in the neighbourhood we do for precisely the same reasons. And for those very same reasons we choose a company to work for. Having chosen our paper, club, neighbourhood, etc., we are then appealed to as part of that value structure. Cars are a classic example of goods deliberately marketed to reinforce the image we have of ourselves, and the values that we represent.

So if we have values which have clear external representations how do we know when we look at a club or company, for example, how well we would fit in? How do we know that they are 'our sort of people'? Basically through perception. All of us have stereotype views of people who belong to certain groups. They either attract us to or repel us from those groups. We make sweeping generalizations about groups and do so primarily through observation of *what* people do and *how* they do it.

If we like what we see, then we want to belong. It appeals to our values. If we want to belong, then we start to behave in a way which we think will make us more acceptable. Just think of the interview you had when you joined your current employers. No doubt you ensured that as much as possible you were 'their kind of person', that you would fit. However, much as we think we will fit, we all have to go through a process of learning and adjustment when we have been accepted. We are still on trial, so to speak. We have to demonstrate our ability to conform to the rules – and as we all know it is the unwritten rules as often as not which are the more important.

In my own training, the way we were managed by one former employer led us to understand immediately that detail and thoroughness were major values for the company. Why? Because from the top down everyone I came into contact with read and approved anything prepared by their subordinates before it went out and all of them had stories relating to those who had committed some awful misdeed in respect of not being thorough. There was nothing in official company policy that said, 'We believe in detail-consciousness.' But everyone knew it was important, primarily through actions like that. What does it say about the management culture? What the company had set up informally was a value that dominated the management process. A value that, most of us now recognize, if it dominates slows decisions, breeds bureaucracy and means that decisions are always delegated upwards rather than down. Everyone checked everyone else.

If we take the issue of detail and thoroughness further we can see that most businesses face a similar challenge: how do we inculcate the highest possible standards into those who work with us whilst giving everyone the highest levels of personal respons-ibility that they can manage? How can we make the learning process relating to standards a positive and empowering one, rather than a negative and belittling one?

It is not only what you do and say publicly, therefore, that sets a culture. A company can have a public culture – what it says it is – and a private culture – what it really is. On joining another previous employer I heard one very clear message from my rela-tives and friends: they do not have a reputation for long-term people development. Yet their publicity and their clear message to me was entirely the opposite. In fact, my five years there were highly developmental and provided me with more challenge than many of my previous roles. But despite this most of the oppor-tunities I was given came more by accident than by design. During my time with the company it replaced or made redundant count-less high-quality managers for a whole variety of reasons, the majority of which had more to do with face fitting than per-formance or ability. Despite the fine words, then, I was convinced by the time I left that my friends and relatives were right. The key point here is that actions speak louder than words.

Culture, then, not only relies on how we act. The other key factor is what management systems and processes we employ in our business to support how we want to act. We can't, for example, claim to encourage our people to act independently if we introduce a budget control process that requires us to get senior management approval for all invoices.

I appreciate culture is not an easy thing to simplify but if I were to draw a representation of organizational culture it would probably be that developed by United Distillers which is shown in Figure 8.2, values, determining our working practices, being demonstrated by how we do things.

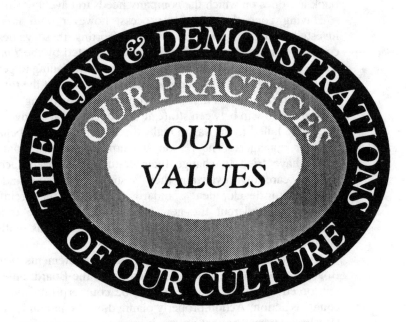

Figure 8.2 The corporate culture as seen at United Distillers

A company culture, therefore is a set of values, and a value is something the organization believes in so strongly that it colours all the choices that we make and actions that we take.

THE IMPORTANCE OF VALUES

Values are very important in understanding how an organization works and why its managers work in particular ways. A value that is held by an organization is a particular belief that it demonstrably puts into action. This is where we strike a dichotomy in much of our industry and public sector. Most of us work for organizations which, strategically, have seen the need for values and operating principles which will take the business forward. As stated in

Chapter 5, some of these like ethics and environmental statements will have arisen because of outside pressure. Others such as respect for people and their development will have come from internal pressures and from recognition that the issues raised earlier in this book are ones on which the company needs to have a position.

Having gone through this process, however, and no doubt invested much in publicizing and supporting these values, few companies have changed. Why? A study quoted by the *Financial Times*[2] found that one of the biggest reasons for failing to generate a substantial climate of success was that the people at the top 'were pulling strategic levers that didn't connect with anything.... There is a very clear gap between strategic and operational change.' What they have failed to do was to make a real impact on the behaviour of their managers. The reason is simple. Very few companies which have tried to change their culture have been successful without carefully reviewing their systems, processes and their reward and development standards to ensure they reinforced rather than undercut the new behaviours they were trying to establish as 'the way we do things around here'. Pious sentiments are fine; they do not often lead to concrete results.

All this means doing more than issuing statements from the Board. Indeed quite often a statement from the Board, unless it is reinforced by Board behaviour, can be counterproductive. What counts is action. Action properly planned, well communicated and clearly signposted so that no one is in any doubt as to what you are doing, why you are doing it and – most important of all – what is in it for them. Why action? Because a value is something you believe in, that you put into action. Until you change the way you do something no one will believe you mean it: what is interesting is that in respect of culture it is not necessarily the big changes that make the real impact. Small shifts in recruitment policies, changes in materials stocked in the stationary cupboard, the circulation of management meeting minutes wider than attendees are all the sorts of things that signal much bigger changes in attitudes and values. And anyway, action is something managers do best ...

CREATING A CLIMATE OF SUCCESS

Creating an organizational climate where a business can sustain a competitive advantage in the longer term is as much about managers behaving in line with the company's values as it is about the exact values themselves. Precisely which values your organization aspires to will be reflected up to a point in the industry and competitive position that it finds itself in. The management task is to develop a sense of common purpose and direction such that every individual gives their commitment and not just their physical presence.

The values that you take from reading this book will, on the whole, be those that your organization probably aspires to: developing people, highest standards of performance, etc. Others may well be new, not on the agenda yet or recognized as issues but not really built into the value structure: ethics, the environment and learning, for example. However, the real differences will start to emerge as you consider the *actions* you have started or planned to address as a result of working through the stocktakes.

Those actions that challenge current culture as it is recognized will be the most difficult to carry out. If there is a 'published' culture to which the actions can be related there is a much better chance of success. The best opportunities are for those actions which reinforce and develop a culture that is already in place or being directed into place from above.

Success breeds success and the purpose of any changes developed as a result of the stocktake process is to add value to the overall business such that it builds a competitive advantage. Starting and succeeding will allow you to develop your action plans and to widen your influence so that you can begin to prompt changes in other areas.

All this means that change in these respects is a long-term process. There is no instant solution. I spent two years trying to recruit a person with disabilities into an organization and, despite all the enthusiasm at our end, failed. Even when success is proved it can be difficult to export. My job-share secretaries were, according to some of my colleagues, 'exceptional' ... so they did not count as a real job-share! Patience and a long-term view are qualities that a self-reliant manager must develop. We will not achieve all our aims overnight, even if we are blessed with a very enlightened chief executive.

STOCKTAKE 14: WHAT CULTURE WAS IT I WAS WORKING FOR
ANYWAY?

It is therefore important that you understand the culture you
work in before you set about taking actions in areas which
are closely aligned with that culture. This stocktake is a
means of reviewing the current state as you see it and to
allow you to identify the gaps between the aspiration and the
reality.

■ The first task is to list what the values are. If there is a
published statement or list then note it below. If not this
is the time to find out. Ask your own functional director
or, better still, the chief executive

1

2

3

4

5

etc.

■ Is there anything that you think should be on the list? If
so do you know why it isn't?

1

2

3

4

5

etc.

■ Against each value in turn identify up to three
management practices or policies which clearly reflect it
and up to three which do not

	Value	Positive demonstrations	Negative demonstrations
1			
2			
3			
4			
5			
etc.			

■ Check your action plans against each of the negative demonstrations and list those for which you have proposals

1

2

3

4

5

etc.

■ List those for which you have no action. Can you think of something you could do, or something that you could influence someone else to do?

	Negative demonstration	Action	By whom
1			
2			
3			
4			
5			
etc			

> ■ Looking at the above, list each of the stocktake action plans in order of priority, putting that which you believe you would achieve most easily at the top
>
> *Priority number*   *Stocktake number*
>
> 1
>
> 2
>
> 3
>
> 4
>
> 5
>
> etc.

UNDERSTANDING YOUR OWN IMPACT

The impact of management behaviour on an organization is constantly underestimated. Behaviour sets the culture, as it is the demonstration of the values held by the business. If the business tolerates a particular kind of management style then *that* represents its culture.

This is very important when considering the major changes facing businesses today. The vast majority of these issues require us to think differently about how we manage people – they require us to adapt our own behaviour if we are going to make any real advance against our major competitors.

Changing behaviour requires skill development, changes to systems and changes to management processes. Without these changes the people who work for us will not accept that we really mean what we say in respect of their value and our commitment to their development. We will fail to gain their commitment. Failing to gain their commitment will mean they will not perform to their full potential and we will not achieve a sustainable competitive advantage.

Conclusion

Self-reliance is more than just a useful heading under which to explore the major people issues facing businesses as we look towards the next century. It is an attempt to get managers to assume ownership and take responsibility for the way in which their businesses develop and progress. This is the challenge of leadership. It is the ability to show clear vision and to demonstrate clear values. It is the ability to take the decision in advance of the trend rather than in response to events. Many different companies have grabbed at the phrase 'Think global, act local' but this is a key component of self-reliance. The ability to understand the big picture and translate it into relevant action in your own area of responsibility is absolutely essential in dealing with the issues raised in this book.

I make no claim to originality of thought, but to me management is about keeping it simple and getting it right as a consequence. There are some very simple and self-evident consequences of not addressing these issues in a positive manner. There are some very simple and straightforward actions and approaches that could be adopted which would enhance an organization's capability to compete successfully:

■ Understandig core competences and working hard to achieve the highest standards
■ Introducing the concept of continuous learning as the major tool for developing people and for encouraging risk and creativity
■ Broadening the pool from which skilled recruits are drawn and changing working patterns to maximize the individual's ability to contribute

- Exploiting the potential of information systems to improve management processes and to build real added-value links from suppliers right through to customers
- Taking a rigorous approach to environmental and ethical obligations and employing this as a competitive weapon in the marketplace
- Flattening and increasing the flexibility of organization structures
- Developing new management styles that can maximize the advantages of a learning culture in a flexible organization

The only constant we will face over the next decade or so will be change. Organizations which take steps similar to those covered here will, I believe, be in a far stronger position to respond quickly and effectively to whatever change throws their way. For what they will have done is moved away from control as a management philosophy towards one based on gaining the commitment of all the individuals who work for them. Committed individuals are far more positive, take far more personal responsibility, are far more self-reliant. This means that they will know what to do, not have to wait until the organization responds.

Setting off down this route with all your action plans and the challenge of your current organization culture can be a daunting prospect. It does take the leadership qualities I referred to earlier, and being a leader means that it may become at times a rather lonely crusade. Miyamoto Musashi, one of the great Japanese strategists of the seventeenth century, wrote:

> 'Crossing at a ford' means, for example, crossing the sea at a strait, or crossing over a hundred miles of broad sea at a crossing place. I believe this 'crossing at a ford' occurs often in a man's lifetime. It means setting sail even though your friends stay in harbour, knowing the route, knowing the soundness of your ship and the favour of the day. When all the conditions are met, and there is perhaps a favourable wind, or a tail wind, then set sail. If the wind changes within a few miles of your destination, you must row across the remaining distance without sail.
>
> If you attain this spirit, it applies to every day life. You must always think of crossing at a ford.[1]

This is the challenge for the self-reliant manager. They must have developed a keen sense of direction and purpose even when others are less sure or going another way. They must be able to share that vision with those they work for and with, as well as those who work for them. In sharing and arguing for that vision they will give leadership. In leading they will, eventually, win.

— Notes and further reading

CHAPTER 2

1   Adam, G., Brewster, C. and Syrett, M., *The Price Waterhouse Cranfield Project on International Strategic Human Resource Management*, Price Waterhouse, 1990.
2   Ibid., 1991.
3   Stephen Duckworth is a consultant specializing in the recruitment and development of people with disabilities. His consultancy is called Disability Matters and is based in London.
4   Adam *et al.*, 1991.

Further reading

Naisbitt, J. and Aburdene, P., *Megatrends 2000: the next ten years – major changes in your life and world*, Sidgwick & Jackson, 1990.
Handy, C., *The Age of Unreason*, Arrow, 1990.

CHAPTER 3

1   Ball, C., *Learning Pays: The Role of Post-compulsory Education and Training, Interim Report*, RSA, 1991.
2   Argyris, C.S., 'Teaching Smart People How to Learn', *Harvard Business Review*, May/June 1991.

Further reading

Pedlar, M., Burgoyne, J. and Boydell, T., *The Learning Company – a strategy for sustainable development*, McGraw-Hill, 1991.
Garrett, B., *The Learning Organisation*, Fontana, 1987.

CHAPTER 4

1   Kotter, J. and Heskett, J., *Corporate Culture and Performance*, Free Press, 1992.

Further reading

Mintzberg, H., *Structure in Fives – designing effective organisations*, Prentice Hall, 1983.

CHAPTER 5

1   Gapper, J., 'Warning over shift in job values', *Financial Times*, Friday 26 October 1990.
2   Trapp, R., 'Companies learn ethics of survival', *Independent on Sunday*, Business Section, Sunday 8 November 1992.
3   Hotten, R., 'Firms reveal they put profits before ethics', *Independent on Sunday*, Business Section, Sunday 3 January 1993.

Further reading

At this stage I am unaware of any books specifically aimed at these areas for managers, but as part of this series Suzanne Pollack will be producing a book on the environment.

CHAPTER 6

1   Howard, R., 'Values make the company: an interview with Robert Hass', *Harvard Business Review*, September–October 1990.

Further reading

Savage, C.M., *Fifth Generation Management*, Digital Press, 1990.

CHAPTER 7

1   Irvin, R.A. and Michaels, E.G., 'Core skills: doing the right things right', *McKinsey Quarterly*, summer 1989.
2   This question forms part of a broader coaching process derived from work done by The Alexander Corporation and particular acknowledgement for the coaching elements in this book are due to Myles Downey and Charles Sherno who have worked closely with United Distillers in their coaching work.
3   Murlis, H. and Wright, A., 'Rewarding the performance of the eager beaver', *Personnel Management*, June 1985.
4   Greg Spiro of Greg Spiro Associates deserves recognition here for his influence in helping form a coherent approach to the process and management of feedback.

Further reading

Boyatzis, R.E., *The Competent Manager*, Wiley & Sons, 1982.

CHAPTER 8

1   This is not the place to enter into a discussion on the art of managing change and the subject is very well covered in Carnell, C., *Managing Change*, Routledge, 1992, in the same series as this book.

2   Lorenz, C. 'Juggling lots of balls in the air ...', *Financial Times*, Management Section, Wednesday 9 January 1991.

Further reading

Handy, C., *Understanding Organisations*, Penguin, 1985.

CONCLUSION

1   Harris, V. (trans), *A Book of Five Rings*, Allison & Busby, 1974.